Those Were the Days

WEIRD & WACKY
ADS
OF YESTERYEAR

[Original endpaper]

[Original endpaper]

Those Were the Days
WEIRD & WACKY ADS OF YESTERYEAR

Compiled by Floyd Clymer

With a New Introduction by
Paul Dickson

DOVER PUBLICATIONS, INC.
Mineola, New York

Bibliographical Note

Those Were the Days: Weird and Wacky Ads of Yesteryear is an unabridged republication of the work originally published as *Floyd Clymer's Historical Scrapbook: Early Advertising Art* by Bonanza Books, New York, in 1955. The endpapers from the 1955 paperback edition appear in the Dover edition on pages iv and v. A new Introduction by Paul Dickson has been specially prepared for the Dover edition.

Library of Congress Cataloging-in-Publication Data

Clymer, Floyd, 1895–1970.
    [Floyd Clymer's scrapbook]
    Those were the days: weird and wacky ads of yesteryear / compiled by Floyd Clymer ; with a new introduction by Paul Dickson.
        p. cm.
    "Unabridged republication of the work originally published as Floyd Clymer's scrapbook : early advertising art, by Bonanza Books, New York, in 1955. The endpapers from the 1955 paperback edition appear in the Dover edition on pages iv and v. A new introduction has been specially prepared for this edition"—T.p. verso.
    ISBN-13: 978-0-486-47242-3
    ISBN-10: 0-486-47242-6
    1. Commercial art—United States—History. 2. Advertising—United States—Specimens. I. Title.

NC998.5.A1C55 2009
741.6'70973—dc22

2009029291

Manufactured in the United States by Courier Corporation
47242601
www.doverpublications.com

Introduction to the Dover Edition

Floyd Clymer (1895–1970) became a celebrity at the age of eleven, when it was discovered that he was the nation's youngest automobile dealer, representing, among other brands, the Cadillac. Many articles were written about this enterprising pre-teen.

He was a pioneer in the sport of motorcycling, not only as a leading motorcycle racer, but also as a dealer, distributor, and, ultimately, a manufacturer who single-handedly tried to revive the iconic Indian motorcycle brand during the 1960s, when he oversaw the manufacture of several different machines that bore that proud name. Clymer opened his first Harley-Davidson dealership while still in his teens, and was also a publisher of motorcycle magazines and a racing promoter. He loved Hollywood, and in his twenties he moved from Colorado to Los Angeles, where he helped promote motorcycling in the 1930s by lending bikes to the movie studios for use in chase scenes. He is now enshrined in the Motorcycle Hall of Fame.

Clymer was also a prolific publisher of automotive ephemera. In the mid 1940s, perhaps unwittingly, he created a new genre. He simply assembled a selection of advertisements, photos, statistics, and articles on old cars into a single volume called *Floyd Clymer's Historical Motor Scrapbook*, pricing it at $1.50. According to a 2005 profile of Clymer in *Hemmings Classic Car* magazine, "In the early Forties, magazines covering automotive history were all but nonexistent in the United States. His widely distributed opening volume created a sensation, earning Clymer a glowing 1944 book review in *Time* and written testimonials from luminaries including California governor Earl Warren, Charles W. Nash and Orville Wright."

More than 150 scrapbooks and other reference books on cars and motorcycles of earlier decades followed, and Clymer was soon cited as a catalyst for the emerging hobby of collecting and restoring antique automobiles and motorcycles. Other publishers soon followed with their own collections of old ads and line art.

Clymer, who had collected ads since his childhood, was still enamored with advertising when he produced *Floyd Clymer's Historical Scrapbook: Early Advertising Art* in 1955. It was another hit. In his disarming introduction he pointed out that he still read the ads first when opening a magazine, but complained that modern advertisements contained "too much white space"—definitely not a problem with this book, which is as cluttered and chaotic as the original Motor Scrapbook.

Part of the attraction of *Those Were the Days: Weird and Wacky Ads of Yesteryear*, this Dover reprint of the 1955 edition, is that the world has changed as much between 1955 and today as it did between the turn of the century and 1955, when the original book came out—so, once again, it serves as a time capsule. One can look at who has survived in these last fifty years. There are ads for companies that are still with us, such as Ford, Proctor and Gamble, and Heinz. There are ads for products that are still available, such as Baker's chocolate, Durkee's dressing, Ivory soap, and Johnson's wax, but Oldsmobile, for instance, is no longer, nor are most of the instant cures and patent medicines.

In addition, there are ads in this book that pose more questions than answers. What was the secret of NO-TO-BAC, which promised to allow one to give up tobacco and "restore man-hood" for 50 cents, and how did Pillsbury's VITOS breakfast cereal "not heat up the blood"? What about the Keeley Cure's "Double-Chloride-of-Gold Treatment," which purported to rid one of addiction to alcohol, opium, or tobacco?

Equally fascinating is the overblown copy that was written to extol the virtues of the most humble products. In this regard, my personal favorite is the ad for Dennison's Crepe paper on page 190, which makes the decorative paper seem as if it has magic powers: "This wonderful paper, in every color and hue is the very embodiment of art and from a few rolls can be created a veritable fairyland of enchantment." Not convinced? "Many are the good-times that owe their delightfulness to the beautiful decorations, festoons, favors and table embellishing, that is easily wrought from Dennison's Crepe Paper."

So, spend more than a few minutes with this book and find those ads that become absolutely compelling for reasons of your own.

—Paul Dickson

Those Were the Days

WEIRD & WACKY
ADS
OF YESTERYEAR

FLOYD CLYMER'S

Scrapbook

Early Advertising Art

•

Bjones, who is fond of his horses, and has had much trouble
with his automobiles, decides to compromise the matter.

[Original title page]

INDEX

2

3

Early Advertising Art
from My Scrapbook

BY FLOYD CLYMER

THIS is a book pertaining to the yesteryears in America, and one of our Scrapbook series which we publish from time to time.

This book includes but a small percentage of the thousands of ads that appeared throughout the years in magazines and newspapers, but the ones shown are typical of the efforts of the early advertising specialists — although many could not really qualify as such.

In reviewing the ads of the past it is evident that the art of advertising has shown progress and, by contrast, the advertisements of today indicate the great strides that have been made in the advertising profession. Many advertisements appearing in this book were published in the days before regulations governing the sale of food, medicines and other merchandise were put into effect by the Government. Many of them would, of course, be refused by publishers of today, and most of the ridiculous advertising claims made in the early days would be taboo under today's Government regulations.

During my lifetime I saved old magazines, photographs, advertisements, catalogs — in fact, anything pertaining to automobiles, motorcycles and other merchandise offered for sale. Having published over 150 books dealing with automotive subjects and cars of the past, I felt that others interested in Americana and the history of our country would enjoy a book of early ad reproductions such as appear in this Scrapbook.

As a youngster I lived in the small town of Berthoud, Colorado, where my father was a physician and surgeon — a general practitioner so common in small towns before the days of the specialists. Dad bought the first automobile to be sold north of Denver in the State of Colorado. It was a 5 horsepower single cylinder curved dash Oldsmobile. At the age of 11, I became a dealer for Cadillac, Reo and Maxwell automobiles in this small Colorado town, situated near the foot of the Rocky Mountains in a fertile farming valley some fifty miles north of Denver. In two years I sold 26 new cars. These were the days when automobile dealer licenses and elaborate salesrooms were unnecessary. In 1906 so many different makes of automobiles were manufactured that almost anyone could secure a car agency by purchasing one demonstrator. By the sale of a Reo to my dad, a Maxwell to a local merchant and a Cadillac to a farmer, I thus became a dealer for all three makes.

A JACK OF ALL TRADES

Even at an early age, I was keenly interested in advertisements, not only about automobiles but about merchandise of all kinds. In addition to selling automobiles, during summer vacations I delivered the Denver Post, as well as the local newspaper, the Berthoud Bulletin. For two summers I operated the shoe shine stand in Purcell's barber shop. Here I met, especially on Saturdays, many farmers who were automobile prospects and I never lost an opportunity to talk about Reo, Maxwell or Cadillac cars. Shoe shines were a nickel — and, in addition to my shine stand, one of my duties at the barber shop was to take care of the bathtub and keep it clean. The local farm hands came in on Satur-

COLORADO LAD YOUNGEST AUTOMOBILE DEALER IN THE WORLD.

Berthoud, Colorado, boasts of the youngest automobile agent in the United States, and that means the world. J. F. Clymer, eleven years old, who has sold thirteen machines in two years who represents the Reo, Maxwell and Cadillac cars, is the little hustler, and declares that he has "Teddy Roosevelt's assurance" that he is the youngest agent in the business.

FLOYD CLYMER, Berthoud, Colo.
The youngest automobile dealer in the world. He is eleven years old and has sold thirteen machines in the past two years.

Like all good dealers, Master Clymer keeps in touch with the trade through a subscription to Motor Field. He sends his favorite magazine a business like announcement which reads as follows:

NOTICE.

I will continue to do business during 1907 at my old office with Dr. J. B. Clymer, and can supply your wants in repairs and supplies, and can save you money.

Remember, I sell the famous Reo, the Maxwell and the Cadillac. See me for prices and terms. Yours truly,

J. F. CLYMER, the Kid Agent.

BUICK INVADING EUROPE.

The Buick motor car compay, by reason of extensive additions to its factories expects to double its output the coming season, and is turning its attention to the European market. John L. Poole has been chosen as Foreign sales manager and leaves for Paris at once.

MITCHELL CATALOG ATTRACTIVE.

The Mitchell Motor Car Company of Racine, Wis., is mailing a very pleasing catalog of 1907 models which is a very attractive example of artistic and tasteful color work.

FROM MOTOR FIELD MAGAZINE..

1907

day, and the price of a bath was 25c. I got 10c for cleaning out the tub, issuing a towel and some soap to each of these grimy hands who were in for their weekly clean-up. Even though Dad was Mayor of the town and the leading doctor, nothing was beneath my dignity when it came to making any kind of sale or doing any kind of work that came my way. I was an ambitious kid.

THESE WERE THE GOOD OLD DAYS

These were the days when ice cream sodas were 5c, Arbuckles Four X Coffee sold for 15c a pound, and a good meal at the local hotel could be had for 25c. A new-fangled dish called the "banana split", with pecan halves soaked in maple syrup, cost 10c. Tariff to the movie show (sometimes called a nickelodeon) was 5c. The Keystone Kops and the Perils of Pauline were feature serials. The localite who pumped the music player (automatic piano) using a roll of paper with holes in the proper places, got 50c a night. That's about the only part time job in Berthoud that I didn't have at one time or another.

I recall the excellent oyster supper that was served in the Grandview Hotel each New Year's Eve, and the cost for the evening was 25c. Most of the townspeople and many farmers turned out for this one grand celebration of the year — the Volunteer Fireman's Annual Ball held in Fairburn's Hall above Andy Fairburn's lumber yard. Dad (as Mayor) and Mother headed up the Grand March. What gala occasions these New Year's balls were — and the kids could stay up until after midnight.

VIRGINIA CHEROOTS, CUBEBS AND SAPOLIO

Louis Greenland, son of the depot agent, was a good friend of mine and usually on Saturday and Sunday mornings the train from Denver brought in jugs of low-priced whiskey, which some of the localites would pick up on arrival. These shipments always came in plain packages, and Louie was kept busy for at least and hour after every train arrived on Saturday night and Sunday morning. Occasionally one of the town drunks was sent to Denver to take the Keeley cure, which was the early day method of breaking the drink habit.

These were also the days of cork-tipped cigarettes, Cubebs, Virginia Cheroots, Sapolio, Horseshoe and Star Chewing Tobacco.

Dozens of ads appeared in the Denver Post, claiming cures for cancer, tuberculosis, baldness, dropsy, rheumatism and nearly every other ailment that befell the human body.

PEDDLERS, STOCK SALESMEN AND BOX SOCIALS

The traveling photographer always visited our town three or four times a year to take photos of the townspeople and the school children. At least one medicine man made our town every week — and I recall some substantial local men who sold Sayman's and Watkins' home remedies by calling on the local residents — in fact, these house-to-house salesmen were the fore-runners of the present day Fuller Brush man. Also, there were many fly-by-night stock salesmen who visited our town to sell worthless mining stocks to the local population and, of course, this was in the days before the Federal Securities Act became law. Their motto was "Let the buyer beware!"

McCormick's, and Davis & Hartford, were two of the local general merchandise stores and they offered a full line of pot-bellied stoves, home coffee grinders, Baker's Cocoa, ice cream freezers, Skat, Perline, Quaker

YOUNG AUTO AGENT DEMONSTRATES MAXWELL

Our cartoonist stopped off at Berthoud while touring northern Colorado last week. He gives his impression of Floyd Clymer the 11-year-old Maxwell dealer "talking up" the Maxwell to a prospect. He operates Berthoud Auto Co. and carries supplies in stock. *Motor Field Magazine (Denver) 1907.*

If are you not particular about your plug equipment,—if any old spark plug will do,— then we cannot hope to interest you in

Breech-Block Plugs

But if you want the best spark plug procurable,—one that is as near soot-proof as it is possible to make plugs; one that for all-round satisfaction cannot be surpassed. We have it for you in the BREECH-BLOCK, with terminal clip handle. It takes only four seconds to remove, clean and replace the BREECH-BLOCK PLUG, and the handle will be found most convenient when testing the spark or removing clip from plug.

If you once use a BREECH-BLOCK you will always use them. That's why we want you to send for sample.

½ STANDARD

The Standard Company, Torrington, Conn.

Oats, Studebaker wagons and Oliver and Moline ploughs. Actually, the farmer could do about all of his shopping in either of these stores, and the prices were extremely low.

One of the pleasures I enjoyed occasionally was going down to McCormick's and operating the coffee grinder. Unground coffee came in paper bags or in bulk instead of in tins. Ed McCormick was a mechanically-minded chap, so he rigged up a portion of a bicycle frame with a set of stationary handlebars and when one sat on the seat and pedaled this stationary bicycle, a chain turned the coffee grinder. Most of the customers wanted their coffee ground and the kids around town, including myself, would take turns and sit on this bicycle anxiously awaiting the next customer so that they could pedal for three or four minutes to grind the coffee.

Lodge members who belonged to such fraternal organizations as the Odd Fellows, Masons, Knights of Columbus, Elks, Moose and the Woodmen of the World had much to do with the advancement of social activities in the community, and several of the big events of the year were the box socials. The women would prepare elaborate food, pack it in attractive boxes with fancy trimmings and, to raise money for their activities, the boxes would be auctioned off to the highest bidder. The bidder was then entitled to eat with his own or someone else's girl or wife. These social events were usually followed by square dancing — which has again become popular in certain parts of the country.

Our car engines were sometimes repaired by the local plumber, Andy Berglin — and, when the springs broke on the rough dirt roads (which was quite often) blacksmiths Bimson or Preston would do a nice job of welding for about a dollar per spring.

In those early days the harness maker, of course, always had a wooden horse on exhibition in his store, displaying a set of harness of the brand he sold or made by hand. And the cigar store owner had the wooden Indian on his sidewalk, which was just as much a trademark of his profession as the colored striped revolving pole used by the barbers to advertise their business.

AUTO DEALER DOUBLES AS PRINTER'S DEVIL

A man by the name of Hardesty published the Berthoud Bulletin and his head man was a tall, likeable fellow by the name of Sam Finley. Sam was about 6'3" tall and as skinny as a beanpole. He and my father were good friends and both expert checker players, and both occasionally went to Denver and other nearby towns to play in tournaments. Sam spent some evenings each week playing checkers with my Dad in his office. In those days the small town doctor usually came back to his office after supper and took care of patients up until 8:00 or 9:00 at night (office calls were $1.50). I liked Sam and Sam liked me, and, as a result, I became sort of a printer's helper or "printer's devil." During the time I sold automobiles I always found time to visit often with Sam at the Bulletin office. One of the first errands Sam asked me to perform was to go to the local machine shop for a "left-handed" monkey wrench — a stunt I later played on other kids in town. A practical joker, Sam was also my teacher the first time I ever went "snipe" hunting, and I later pulled the trick on many another unsuspecting "snipe" hunter.

I claim to be the only automobile dealer — either past, present, living or dead — who ever performed the following combined operations: wrote

NOTICE TO ALL AUTO PROSPECTS

THE REO is the BEST of all AUTOS for use in Colorado.

1 or 2 cylinder models. Both have good power for the mountains (go to Estes Park with ease—climb the steep Rapids Hill with no pushing).

Demonstration any time—I have a one-cylinder model now to demonstrate and a two-cylinder 5-passenger model (with removable tonneau) will be here next week.

NEW OWNERS THAT BOUGHT REOS OF ME

ask them—they will tell you how fine the Reo is. REO OWNERS THIS YEAR are Bob Kahler, John Whowell, Zenas McCoy, Fred Bein and Dr. McFadden of Loveland.

NEW MAXWELL OWNERS

Ed McCormick, Charley Breon, who will operate Berthoud Auto Livery, Elmer Hankins and Cy Waite of Johnstown.

NO CADILLAC SALES

lately as people seem to want 2-cylinder cars now.

See me before you buy any auto as I will take any prospects for any car to Denver and they can compare all makes —and I'll surely get the order for a Maxwell, Reo or Cadillac —the best of all cars—we can prove it—See me.

ALWAYS REMEMBER

I have carbide, Zeroline, Mobiloil, 600W (for steamers), Weed Tire Chains, Firestone and Diamond Tires (also agent for Swinehart solid tires), Solar and Rushmore Lamps, windshields and tops on special order to fit any automobile.

FLOYD CLYMER
the 12 year old Kid Agent
for Reo cars.

Agent for Motor Age and
Motor Field Magazines

Complete service for the
automobilist.

FLOYD CLYMER,
PROP.

BERTHOUD
Auto Co.

Office in
Dr. J. B. Clymer Building
Berthoud, Colorado

This ad appeared in the Berthoud Bulletin — 1907

his own advertising, set up his own ad in type, operated the printing press to print the paper, and either delivered the papers to the local subscribers in person or took them to the post office for mailing.

FIFTEEN HOURS EXCHANGED FOR A $1.80 AD

I did this for about two years and, being intrigued with the job, I was valuable enough to Mr. Hardesty that he ran one ad for me about my auto business in the Bulletin, in return for all of the odd jobs I did at the Bulletin office. I learned to hand-set the type, and each character was neatly tucked away in a little tray. The type setter had to learn to read the type in an upside-down position, which I did. I later figured out that, had I paid the going rate of 15¢ a column inch for my ads, instead of working about 15 hours a week, the average ad that I ran would have cost me about $1.80 — but I had a lot of fun and enjoyed this work. The worst moments I had were when Sam occasionally handed me an ad to set up for my competitors — George Nall, who sold Fords, or Lew Hertha, the Stanley Steamer dealer. I always thought Sam gave me this job to needle me rather than set the type himself, which he could have done blindfolded in half the time. Sam was an expert typesetter — I was an amateur.

Every Friday night Sam and I would work late to get the Bulletin off the old flat-bed press, which I think must have been an early Meihle. It took us only about three hours after the paper was locked up to do the printing and place the names of the subscribers on the papers with an old hand-operated cutter that put the glue on the yellow paper strips and cut the strip at the proper place. Then we rushed them to the Post Office for early morning Saturday delivery. I think the total circulation was about 1,200. But it was an experience that I thoroughly enjoyed and one of the happy periods of my life as an ambitious small town youngster.

Reproduced in this book are two of my ads which appeared in the Bulletin in 1907 and 1908. Readers should remember that both of these were written and set up when I was a 12 and 13-year old kid. The ad layout and the copy are not much worse, really, than several of the other "corny" ads that appear in this book.

TWO YEARS IN THE FOURTH GRADE

Even in my years as a young car dealer advertising intrigued me. I thoroughly enjoyed the hundreds of "free" catalogs about early cars. I wrote for and received many beautiful catalogs from the early automobile manufacturers. Of the 2200 different makes of cars at one time or another since the inception of the automotive industry in our country I must have received at least one catalog of each make. There were 125 different makes of steam cars, 120 electrics, 122 Cyclecars (the tiny narrow tread ones of 1913-14-15 era). There were a hundred or more makes driven by single or double chains, and friction transmission makes. The battle raged between cars using planetary or sliding gear transmissions. Air cooled engine devotees ridiculed the water-cooled engine cars. Makers of high-wheeled cars with buggy-type wheels and solid rubber tires fought a battle with ones having smaller wheels and pneumatic tires. Even the makers could not decide whether the rear entrance should be on the side or a door in the rear, and whether the rear tonneau should be a permanent or a detachable part of the body. Engines of the 2-cycle type with no valves were favored by some over the conventional 4-cycle engine with valves. One 2-cycle engine exponent, the

NOTICE TO ALL AUTO PROSPECTS

I HAVE BEEN TO CHEYENNE, WYO.

to see the great New York-to-Paris racers go through Cheyenne in the wonderful race.

MAYBE YOU KNOW

that the famous E. Linn Mathewson of Denver, who has made me his Reo agent here in Berthoud, is one of the relay race drivers of the Thomas Flyer in the big race.

I RODE IN THE FAMOUS THOMAS FLYER

at Cheyenne last week when Linn Mathewson tested the car to start over mountains of the Continental Divide to Laramie and Rawlins then to Salt Lake City. It is a wonderful racer—better than all others, I think.

I AM NOW A THOMAS-FLYER AGENT

by authority of Linn Mathewson, distributor of Reo and Thomas-Flyer cars in Denver. He told me to also act as his Thomas agent, as well as Reo agent in Berthoud and Johnstown, and maybe I'll also have Loveland territory. He will see later on after the race.

THOMAS-FLYER PROSPECTS SHOULD SEE ME

for a new Thomas-Flyer and prices. Ask me for a catalogue. Demonstration can be arranged next month when Mr. Mathewson will be here in latest model Thomas-Flyer.

FLOYD CLYMER
the 13 year old Kid Agent

BERTHOUD AUTO CO.

**Reo, Maxwell and Cadillac Autos
Thomas, Auto-Bi and Yale
Motorcycles**

FLOYD CLYMER —
The Kid Agent
Owner and General Manager

**Office in Dr. J. B. Clymer Building
Berthoud, Colorado**

The above ad appeared in the Berthoud, Colo. Bulletin in 1908

Elmore, built in Clyde, Ohio, actually built and sold cars using one, two, three, four and six-cylinder engines. One, two, four, six and eight-cylinder cars were fighting a hard battle for sales.

As a youngster I eagerly watched these battles as the automobile industry developed. Much of the study I made as an eager beaver car dealer and enthusiast were made during school hours. I had a neat trick of hiding one or two car catalogs each day between the pages of some of my school books. This was my life — I cared not for spelling, history or arithmetic; only those wheezing, rattling, smoking and stinking early autos held my interest.

My dad had a great sense of humor — he always said I liked the fourth grade so much I stayed there two years. To this day I don't know why my efficient and well liked teacher, Blanche Wright, ever put up with me when she taught the third and fourth grades in the Berthoud Public School. She must have liked me for she kept me in her third and fourth grade room for a total of three years.

The best thing I did was to keep the thousands of early ad pages, catalogs, magazines and photos that I started collecting as a kid in grade school. They enabled me to start a publishing business which has compiled and published over 150 books on automotive subjects.

The well-prepared ads by members of the advertising profession of today always interest and intrigue me, but I still think they use too much white space. Many times as I go through a magazine I scan the ads thoroughly before I do any other reading.

The ethics of advertising have been greatly improved. In reading some of the early advertisements that appear in this book, one might conclude that there were no advertising ethics in those early days.

I hope that the readers of this book will find as much enjoyment in reading and looking at the early advertisements as I had in selecting them and compiling the book. This is the first of a series of similar books which will be published from time to time by our firm. We feel that we are performing a service that will be of interest and value to thousands who are interested in preserving records and information pertaining to the art of early day advertising, which played such an important part in a gone but not forgotten era of the past.

Floyd Clymer.

THE J. L. MOTT IRON WORKS,
NEW YORK AND CHICAGO.

1891

Copyright, 1892, by THE J. L. MOTT IRON WORKS.

MOTT'S PATENT DIRECT-ACTION SYPHON JET
WATER-CLOSET,

The Primo.

The Primo is an imported Syphon Jet Water-closet,
warranted not to craze or discolor. The Bowl contains
a large body of water, and there are no mechanical parts
liable to get out of order. When the Pull is drawn
down the Syphon is started and contents of Bowl are
quickly and almost noiselessly ejected. A feature of
the Primo is the great depth of water in the Bowl
which affords an effectual barrier against sewer gas.
Illustrated Price Lists mailed on application.

14

1891

ILLUSTRATED CATALOGUE
20 CENTS

LARGEST ASSORTMENT & LOWEST PRICES

OUR STYLES & PRICES CHALLENGE COMPETITION

STYLISH FURS HATS TOQUES & BONNETS

STYLISH COATS GOWNS CAPES & WRAPS

DEUTSCH & Co.

FIFTH AVE.

COR. 22 ND ST.

MILLINERS, FURRIERS AND TAILORS.

18

The Ladies' Home Journal

1891

⇥————For January.

Now Ready on the News Stands
Ten Cents a Copy.

CONTRIBUTORS

Henry M. Stanley,
Oliver Wendell Holmes,
Ex-President Hayes,
Hon. John Wanamaker,
Joseph Jefferson,
Lawrence Barrett,
Hon. Hannibal Hamlin,
Sarah Orne Jewett,
Charles A. Dana,
General Lew Wallace,
Robert J. Burdette,
Mrs. Margaret Bottome,
James Whitcomb Riley,
George W. Childs,
Will Carleton,
Edward Bellamy,
Mrs. Lyman Abbott,
Julian Hawthorne.

First Installment of Mrs. Whitney's "A GOLDEN GOSSIP." First Paper on "UNKNOWN WIVES OF WELL-KNOWN MEN"—Mrs. Edison, with Portrait. First Paper on "WOMEN'S CHANCES AS BREAD-WINNERS." "QUEEN VICTORIA AT MY TEA-TABLE," by Madame Albani-Gye.

Circulation now exceeds 500,000 copies each issue.

Send $1.00 for 1891 Subscription, and receive the Thanksgiving and Christmas numbers FREE.

VOID

CURTIS PUBLISHING COMPANY., Philadelphia, Pa.

1891

> " Twin roses by the zephyr blown apart,
>   Only to meet again more close, and share
>   The inward fragrance of each other's heart."

So Keats describes the lovers in "Isabella." Many lovers have been separated because the health of the lady in the case failed. No man finds attraction in a woman who is subject to nervous excitability, exhaustion, prostration, hysteria, spasms and other distressing, nervous symptoms, commonly attendant upon functional derangement and organic diseases peculiar to women.

The remedy for all such maladies is Dr. Pierce's Favorite Prescription. As a soothing and strengthening nervine it is unequaled. As an invigorating tonic, it imparts strength to the uterine organs as well as to the whole system. Contains no alcohol to inebriate ; no sugar or syrup to derange digestion ; a legitimate *medicine*, not a *beverage*.

For all displacements, as prolapsus, retroversion, anteversion and flexions, causing weak and aching back, bearing-down sensations, ulceration, unnatural discharges and kindred ailments, the " Favorite Prescription " is an unequaled remedy, and the *only guaranteed* one.

You only pay for *the good* you get in using Dr. Pierce's Favorite Prescription.

Can you ask more ?

World's Dispensary Medical Association, Proprietors, Buffalo, N. Y.

1891

290 Fifth Ave, New York.

L. P. Hollander & Co.
Boylston St·· ··Boston·

[Established 1780.]

"LA BELLE CHOCOLATIÈRE": W. BAKER & CO.'S Registered Trade-Mark.

No Chemicals are used in any of *Walter Baker & Co.'s Chocolate* and *Cocoa Preparations.*

These preparations have stood the test of public approval for *more than one hundred years*, and are the acknowledged standard of purity and excellence.

VOLUME XVII.   NEW YORK, JANUARY 8, 1891.   NUMBER 419.

Entered at the New York Post Office as Second-Class Mail Matter.
Copyright 1891, by MITCHELL & MILLER.

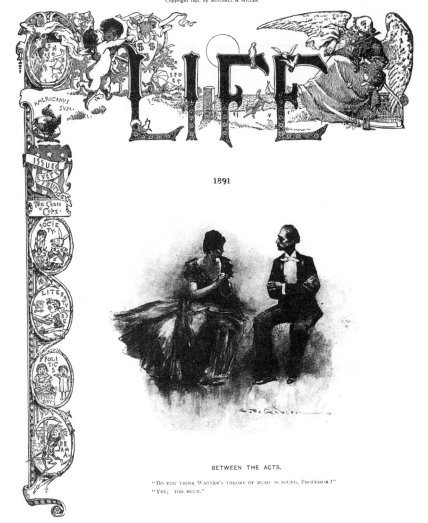

1891

BETWEEN THE ACTS.

"DO YOU THINK WAGNER'S THEORY OF MUSIC IS SOUND, PROFESSOR?"
"YES; TOO MUCH."

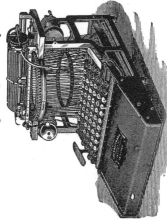

1891

Vegetable Glycerine.

PROCTER & GAMBLE'S VEGETABLE GLYCERINE IS PUT UP IN GLASS-STOPPER BOTTLES
THAT IT ALWAYS MAY BE ON THE TOILET TABLE. THESE BOTTLES ARE OF TWO
SIZES, ONE POUND AND ONE-HALF POUND, AND ARE SOLD AT $1.25 AND 75C.,
RESPECTIVELY.

IF YOUR DRUGGIST DOES NOT KEEP PROCTER & GAMBLE'S VEGETABLE GLYCERINE, IT WILL
BE SENT TO ANY ADDRESS, EXPRESSAGE PREPAID, ON RECEIPT OF PRICE, BY

THE PROCTER & GAMBLE CO.,

GLYCERINE DEPARTMENT,   CINCINNATI, O.

1891

Smokers' Throat:

PROCTER & GAMBLE'S VEGETABLE
GLYCERINE WILL RELIEVE IN-
STANTLY THE DRY, PARCHED
AND BURNING SENSATION THAT
SMOKERS OFTEN FEEL ON THEIR
TONGUE OR IN THEIR THROAT.

FOR PARTICULARS SEE ELEGANT
BOOK OF TOILET RECIPES THAT
CAN BE PREPARED EASILY AND
CHEAPLY AT HOME. SENT TO ANY
ADDRESS FOR TWO TWO-CENT
STAMPS. ADDRESS,

THE PROCTER & GAMBLE CO.,

GLYCERINE DEPARTMENT,   COPYRIGHT, 1891.   CINCINNATI, O.

32

The Portraits of
Healthy Infants
Sent by
Thankful Parents
Offer
Irrefutable Evidence
Of the Excellence of

MELLIN'S FOOD

FOR INFANTS AND INVALIDS.

THE DOLIBER-GOODALE CO., Boston, Mass

Invites correspondence.

BABY MARSH,
Lynn, Mass.

COLONEL ÆSOP, who had recently gone to Sardis to help King Crœsus to pull through some political jobs, went out for a stroll up and down Broadway, the principal thoroughfare of Sardis. When he returned to the palace he related to the King the following story :

An Ass met a Calf one afternoon.

"Aw, deah boy," said the Ass, "you look ill."

"Yaas," answered the Calf; "caught a dweadful cold this mawning."

"My, my!" said the Ass. "Did you sit in a dwaft?"

"Yaas," answered the Calf; "sat wight neah a vulgar fellow who whistled for his dog."

When the distinguished fabler had concluded his story, the King said :

"Æsop, some of your yarns are rather hard to believe. For example, I can hardly imagine asses and calves conversing one with another."

"That brings me to my moral," said Æsop. "Rich men should see that their sons become not asses and calves."—*Detroit Free Press.*

1891

1891

THE
PREVENTOR

AND
HEALER.

Gentlemen who find that Shaving causes irritation, pimples, a drawing, smarting sensation, will find that the use of

"GENUINE YANKEE SHAVING SOAP"

relieves all this. Besides creating a most rich, creamlike lather, which softens the beard and renders shaving very *easy*, it has medicinal properties of pronounced value, and acts gently yet effectively as a preventive and healer of all cutaneous troubles peculiar to the face.

"Yankee Shaving Soap" has enjoyed the confidence of the American people for HALF A HUNDRED YEARS, is standard for quality in the United States Navy, and is known and extensively used throughout the civilized world. Sold by Druggists. One cake (for trial) mailed, postpaid, to any part of the world for 15c. in stamps. Address

THE J. B. WILLIAMS' CO., Glastonbury, Conn.
(Established 1840, as Williams & Bros., Manchester.)

Those who prefer to use Shaving Soap in *Stick* form will find WILLIAMS' SHAVING STICK to contain the same excellent qualities as our "Yankee Soap." Shaving Stick in metallic case, leatherette cover. Soap exquisitely scented with Attar of Roses. Price, 25c.

Try a pound package (6 cakes) of **WILLIAMS' BARBERS' BAR SOAP**, for TOILET USE. So DELICATE. Sent by MAIL for 40c. in stamps, or can be had of any Druggist.

-HARMONY-

1891   ALL MANKIND LOVES A LOVER.   (EMERSON.)

SO DO WE. Spite of what LIFE says, they marry and must have pianos.

Do you notice in this picture the long music desk? It swings out automatically when you uncover the keys—so convenient for duets, or for two or three instruments in concert. One of our many practical patents. Added to first-class work these improvements are surely desirable. You will remember that "we are the people" who have the Soft Stop in our pianos, saving the din of practice, and the wear on both nerves and instrument. Dwellers in apartments ought to be forbidden by law to have any other.

WRITE FOR 100-PAGE CATALOGUE--FREE.

———

WE SHIP ON APPROVAL,

Piano to be returned at our expense for railway freights both ways, if it prove unsatisfactory on trial in your home. Distance makes no difference, 1 mile or 2,000 miles are no more obstacle to us than a city block in Boston. Old pianos taken in exchange and terms of payment to suit your reasonable convenience.

———

IVERS & POND PIANO COMPANY,

MASONIC TEMPLE, 183-186 TREMONT STREET,

BOSTON, MASS.

OUR LATEST STYLES CAN BE SEEN AT

J. G. RAMSDELL'S, 1111 Chestnut St., Philadelphia.
F. H. CHANDLER'S, 300 Fulton St., Brooklyn.
G. W. HERBERT'S, 18 East 17th St., New York.

W. J. DYER & BRO.'S, St. Paul and Minneapolis.
PHILIP WERLEIN'S, 187 Canal St., New Orleans.
SANDERS & STAYMAN'S, Baltimore, Washington and Richmond.

For Pacific Coast, KOHLER & CHASE, San Francisco, Cal.

MELLIN'S FOOD is food, not medicine, and can be instantly prepared whenever quick nourishment is desired, as it requires no cooking. Try two table-spoonfuls in a cup of milk or water, hot or iced, as preferred, and you will be fed, nourished, and strengthened.

A seventy-two page cloth-bound book, telling how to use Mellin's Food, will be sent free to anyone requesting it. DOLIBER-GOODALE CO.

BOSTON, MASS.

REDFERN

1895

ℰ. Redfern

LADIES' TAILOR and COURT DRESSMAKER ~
210 FIFTH AVENUE ~

41

43

1895
WARFARE OF THE FUTURE.

46

New Equipment on the Pennsylvania Limited.

The celebrated Pennsylvania Limited was never so luxurious in all its appointments as it is at present with its splendid equipment of new cars. Every car in the train has just come out of the shops as bright and as fresh as a new coin. This is the only perfectly appointed Limited Train in service between New York and Chicago.

A DOG, on a warm summer day, lay down in the shade, and soon fell asleep. He was awakened by the noise of a huge bull approaching his shady resting-place.

"Get up," said the bull, "and let me lie down there ! "

"No," replied the dog, "you have no right to the place ; I was here first."

"Well," said the bull, looking innocently at the dog, but with a ferocious twinkle in his left eye, which made the dog's spinal column run cold and his lower jaw give way, "let us toss up for it."

"Thank you," said the dog politely, "I never gamble," and he walked away.—*Ex.*

Handsomest Passenger Train in the World.

This is the popular verdict on the Pennsylvania Limited, and one who sees the train now in the brightness and freshness of its new equipment will fully endorse it. The new cars, the compartment car just introduced and the other distinctive features make it the most luxurious train in the world, and the only perfectly appointed Limited Express. It leaves New York at 10.00 A. M. every day for Chicago.

47

Isaac B. Potter, Chief Consul N. Y. State L. A. W., and President Brooklyn Bicycle Club, writes:

" My desire to render a substantial favor to the wheelmen of America impels me to say a good word for Salva-cea. For that lameness of muscles which comes to the moderate rider whenever he attempts a long day's run, I have found nothing to be compared with it; while for sprains and bruises its curative and soothing effects are really magical. I heartily recommend it."

Chafings and Sore Muscles can't last over night if you use   1895

Salva-cea.
(TRADE MARK)

It takes away at once all the pain and stiffness. A little Salva-cea, after a hard day's work or walk or ride, will put you into shape in short order. For Soreness, Strained or Overworked Muscles, the easing of Stiff Joints, Sunburn, and the Bites and Stings of Insects, nothing compares with Salva-cea.

It relieves pain;
Subdues Inflammation;   Allays Irritation.

Two sizes, 25 and 50 cents per box. At druggists', or by mail.

The Brandreth Co., 274 Canal St., New York.

═THE IMPERIAL═
BALL-BEARING AXLE.

1895 PATTERN.

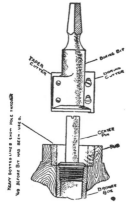

Perfected
Anti-Friction
For Vehicles.

IMPERIAL BOXING BIT.

The Imperial has stood the <u>test</u>.

3,000 sets in use is our strongest recommendation.

Can be used on old or new work.

With our Boxing Bit they can be put on as easy as the regular axle.

Screw the nut up, and your adjustment is <u>perfect</u>.

Our Axle makes absolutely the best Ball-Bearing Vehicle on the market.

Send for Catalogue
and Prices.

**OUR IMPERIAL DUST PROOF
SCREW BASE BANDS.**

Ornamental. Safe. Dust and Water Proof.
For all kinds of Axles.

Imperial Ball-Bearing Axle Co.
CHICAGO, ILL.

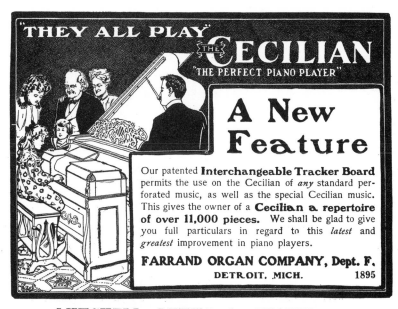
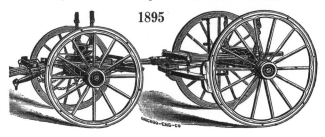

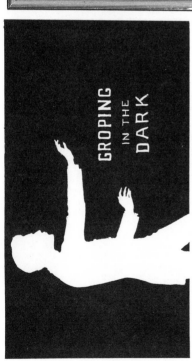
52

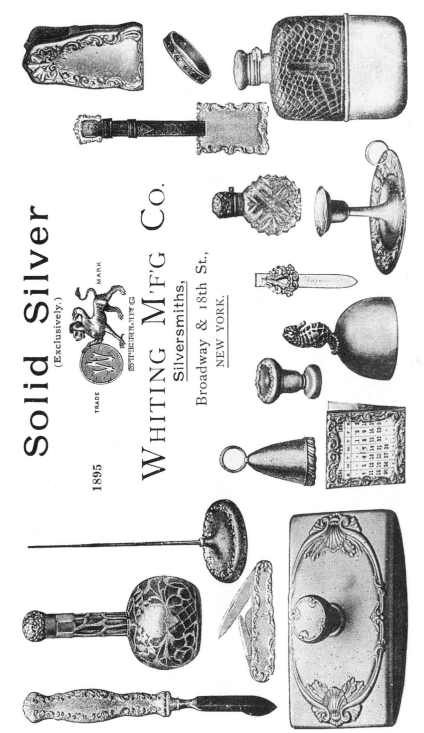

Solid Silver
(Exclusively.)

STERLING

TRADE MARK

1895

WHITING M'F'G CO.
Silversmiths,
Broadway & 18th St.,
NEW YORK.

FASTEST
TIRE ON EARTH
THE GREAT G. AND J.
USED ON ALL
RAMBLERS
ANY DEALER WILL SUPPLY
THEM ON ANY WHEEL
IF YOU INSIST

The RAMBLER will bring back health.

GORMULLY & JEFFERY MFG CO
RIDING
ACADEMIES

1895

Riding any wheel is exercise
Riding RAMBLER BICYCLES is luxurious
exercise.

55

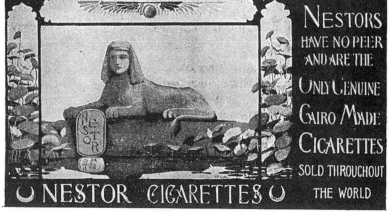

WILLIAMS' SHAVING STICK

1895

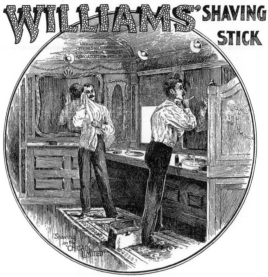

Shaving on the "CHICAGO LIMITED"

"The next time I buy a shaving-stick, it will be

WILLIAMS' SHAVING STICK."

The Soap—is a rich, creamy white—very delicate in odor—and produces a wonderfully soft—cool lather that *never dries on the face* while shaving.

The Case—(patented) is a great favorite. The glove-fitting cover never comes off except when *taken* off. Case never breaks—never leaks. No loose piece of soap rolling about in your satchel.

Enough WILLIAMS' STICKS sold in 1893 to shave over **20,000,000 Men.**

Note—! WILLIAMS' costs no more than others. But—it's *worth* more.

WILLIAMS' SOAPS—*in three*   *principal forms—are sold by all Dealers.*

" Genuine Yankee " Soap, 10c.
Oldest and most famous cake of shaving soap in the world. Millions using it.

Williams' Shaving Stick, 25c.
Strong, metal-lined case. For Tourists' and Travelers' use. Don't fail to ask for WILLIAMS'—and take *no other.*

Williams' Barbers' Soap, 40c.
This is the kind your barber should use. It is also most excellent for Toilet use. Tons of it sold yearly to *families.* 6 cakes in a package—40c.

SPECIAL OFFER—If your dealer does not have these soaps—we mail them—to any address—postpaid on receipt of price.—All three kinds sent for 75c. in stamps.   Address **THE J. B. WILLIAMS CO., Glastonbury, Ct., U. S. A.**
London Office: 64 GREAT RUSSELL ST., W. C.

59

61

62

MONTGOMERY WARD & CO.'S IM-PROVED HIGH ARM SEWING MACHINE

*A STRICTLY HIGH-GRADE Sewing Machine with all modern improvements It has few equals. There are none better. Ten years before the public, with a record of 60,000 machines sold, all giving perfect satisfaction. This is our best evidence of quality. Warranted for **Ten Years**. Shipped subject to a thorough trial. If not satisfactory, return at **our** expense both ways, and we will refund the money without question. We guarantee safe delivery; the purchaser assumes no risk whatever.*

1898

Above Styles crated for Shipment Weight about 120 pounds each

THIS CUT is an exact representation of Montgomery Ward & Co.'s High Arm Sewing Machines Nos. 5 and 5½. Ask us to send **Catalogue F.** It's free. It tells all about prices on Pianos, Organs, and Sewing Machines

OUR PRICES

No. 5. Five drawers, as in cut, walnut woodwork
$19.50

No. 5½. Five drawers as in cut, oak woodwork, very popular
$19.50

No. 6. Seven drawers, three on each side and center drawer, walnut woodwork
$20.50

No. 6½. Seven drawers, three on each side and center drawer, oak woodwork
$20.50

With Every M. W. & Co.'s High Arm Sewing Machine we send a Warranty Certificate as follows:

Certificate of Warranty.

We hereby Warrant this Montgomery Ward & Co. Improved High Arm Sewing Machine numbered.................to endure the natural wear and tear of family use for ten years, and agree to supply free of charge, any defective or broken parts of same for that term, excepting only the wear and breakage of needles, bobbins and shuttles. The results of carelessness in handling or abuse of any kind are not included in this guarantee.

Chicago....................189....   _____   MONTGOMERY WARD & CO.

MONTGOMERY WARD & CO., CHICAGO

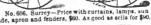

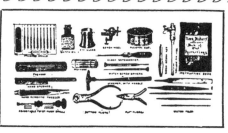

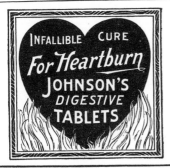

A HINT TO SHREWD BUYERS

THE COLUMBUS YOUNG MEN'S SPECIAL

$47.^{64}
$47.^{64}
$47.^{64}

THE LATEST THING IN BUGGIES. IT IS UP TO DATE. ALL NEW WRINKLES ARE ON THIS RIG. READ THE FOLLOWING DESCRIPTION CAREFULLY AND NOTE ALL THE NEW FEATURES FOR 1898.......TERMS: CASH WITH ORDER

DESCRIPTION

AXLES—⅞-inch double collar.

WHEELS—⅞-inch tread Sarven patent, made of selected second-growth Ohio hickory; round edge steel tire, bolted between every spoke.

GEAR—Hickory, well ironed; Norway iron clips and bolts.

SPRINGS—Oil tempered. Warranted.

BODY—Made of seasoned wood, screwed from inside, glued and plugged; round corner seat, solid panel back. Your choice of either 22 x 52 inches or 24 x 52 inches.

TOP—Leather quarters, rubber cloth lined back curtain, unlined side curtains, padded leather back stays, crimped top lining and stays as shown in cut.

CUSHIONS—Dark green fast color cloth, made up in fancy pleats, spring back, sides of seat padded; fancy tan cord binding around edge of cushion and back.

TRIMMINGS—Patent leather dash, fitted with fancy double rail and silver whip socket, silver hub bands, silver top nuts, silver-nuts on body loops; fancy full length carpet, also carpet on sides and end of body (a new idea, very taking); scrolls on seat risers, two gold stripes full length of body.

PAINTING—Body rich black, finished with Valentine's varnish; gear either black, Brewster green, or carmine, with triple fine line gold striping.

It will attract the attention of every man, woman and child in your town.

We also have the SURPRISE Buggy, $36.25; the CINCINNATI SPECIAL, $42.00;
Our Famous SILVER STAR Buggy, $52.75; and the LEADER Road Wagon, $22.95
All known from the Atlantic to the Pacific.

SEND FOR OUR VEHICLE CATALOGUE.

MONTGOMERY WARD & CO.
CHICAGO

THE MOTO-CYCLE OR HORSELESS CARRIAGE.

The two Electric Horseless Carriages shown here are used by us as advertising novelties, for the purpose of calling attention to our business, which is to sell to farmers, mechanics, and the people generally throughout the country, anything they need or use, and at wholesale prices. We had these two built expressly for our use, at a cost of about $3,000 each, and are sending them to the smaller cities of the Union, so that those who might otherwise never see a Horseless Carriage will have a chance to see and examine the latest and most up-to-date vehicles of the kind.

During the past year our Carriages have been exhibited in Chicago, Madison, St. Paul, DesMoines, Topeka, Fort Worth, Galveston, Houston, Dallas, Atchison, Leavenworth, and St. Joseph, and in hundreds of smaller cities in Illinois, Wisconsin, Minnesota, South Dakota, Iowa, Kansas, Missouri, Arkansas, Indian Territory, Oklahoma, and Texas. At every place where shown they have attracted great attention, and been commented upon in the most favorable manner. They have been ridden in by all classes of people, from the frolicsome school-boy to congressmen, state senators, and governors of various States, all of whom have been delighted with their ride, and admitted it to be one of the most pleasant in their experience.

Montgomery Ward & Co.'s Horseless Carriages.

OUR METHODS OF ADVERTISING.

Advertising-Car "Success."

We have been noted as successful advertisers —as those who receive positive results from appropriations expended for advertising purposes. That we reach the people cannot be denied, for 2,000,000 customers prove that fact. One of our latest ventures in the advertising line is the sending of two very handsome cars on a tour of the United States. No samples are carried on these cars, and no orders are taken by our representatives; they simply paint signs, distribute advertising matter, explain our methods of doing business, and entertain the people of the towns they visit. With these cars are our Horseless Carriages described in this book. The

ADVERTISING-CAR "SUCCESS"

is 55 feet long, 10 feet wide and 14 feet high. It was built at a cost of $10,000. It is divided into kitchen, pantry, buffet, sleeping apartments, and observation room.

The kitchen, occupying one end, is supplied with the latest style "Wilkes" range, large refrigerator, numerous cupboards, sinks and drawers, and all the conveniences of the modern dining car. The central portion of the car is divided into five Pullman sections of double upper and lower berths, affording sleeping accommodations for twenty persons. There are also two sets of closets or wardrobes and toilets in this division. The observation room is 10x16 feet in size, with two side doors, and two doors and window opening on rear platform.

The furnishings are of the Pullman design and the same as found on the regular Pullman sleeper. The car is finished in ash and hard oil, and is heated by the circulating hot water system and lighted by electricity. The trucks are the standard Pullman six-wheel trucks with Allen paper car-wheels and Westinghouse air-brakes.

ADVERTISING-CAR "PROGRESS."

The outside appearance of the advertising-car "Progress" compares favorably with the car "Success"—at the same time the car is not so expensively gotten up, or so handsomely finished in its interior. Our object in buying it was, that our representatives might have a car to carry the things essential to make their journey pleasant and to accomplish the objects of their trip. This car contains the Electric Carriage, a fine gas engine and dynamo for use in charging the batteries which furnish the electric current to propel the carriage, and another set of batteries which supplies electric lights for the two cars. In this car are also carried the commissary supplies, paints. oils, and stencils, souvenir books, pamphlets, specimen catalogues, and all kinds of advertising matter: also the musical instruments, scenery, and other paraphernalia used by those who give our evening entertainments.

Advertising-Car "Progress."

With the permission of Montgomery Ward & Co., we have reproduced the original Montgomery Ward 1898 Almanac and Yearbook. These are now a rare collector's item. We can supply this unusual and interesting book at $1.00 per copy.

73

The "Truth about the Regal" is a compilation of facts that ought to and does interest every wearer of shoes. You should know about the shoes you wear — where they are made and of what and how they are made — this book tells you. We want you to read the "Truth about the Regal" — the booklet is free to you — costs you nothing but a postal. It will interest you.

1899

THE TRUTH ABOUT THE REGAL

KING CALF

TRADE MARK

The **Regal**

Every man in the country knows the Regal Shoe — it's the best made! The price $3.50 alone didn't make it so, but the price has proved a revelation to men who had previously paid two and three times the Regal price for their shoes.

"King Calf" is tanned for and used only in Regal Shoes. "King Calf" is the best leather made. No other shoe manufacturer gets a bit of it. Leather stitched with silk — the best of both — is what Regal Shoes are made of. None better at any price.

Were you to pay for the Regal the customary middlemen's profits, it would cost you $6. We save you these profits, the first time and every time, and the Regal costs you but $3.50. From maker to wearer, and the maker in this case stands back of the Regal.

Send postal for catalogue T, "The Truth about the Regal."

L. C. BLISS & CO., Mail Order Department, 109 Summer Street, Boston.

Delivered prepaid to any address in the United States upon receipt of $3.75 per pair.

Regal Dressing cleans, preserves, and polishes men's, women's, and children's shoes—Russet and Black. Sample size, 15c. postpaid.

At all Stores, **$3.50** per pair.

STORES.

Boston, 109 Summer Street ; Providence, 220 Westminster Street; New York, 115 Nassau Street, 1347 Broadway, 291 Broadway; Brooklyn, 357 Fulton Street, 111 Broadway; Baltimore, 219 E. Baltimore Street ; Philadelphia, 8th and Chestnut Streets ; Washington, D. C., 1003 Penn Ave.; Pittsburg, 309 Fifth Ave.; Buffalo, 362 Main Street ; Cincinnati, 13-15 Fountain Square ; St. Louis, 618 Olive Street ; Chicago, 103 Dearborn Street, 215 Dearborn Street; Detroit, 122 Woodward Ave.; Cleveland, 17 Euclid Ave.; Denver, 423 Sixteenth Street ; Utica, N. Y., 4 La Fayette Street ; Albany, N. Y., 34 Maiden Lane ; Atlanta, Ga., 6 Whitehall Street ; Milwaukee, Wis., 212 Grand Ave.

Factory, Whitman, Mass.

Rugby Russet Oxford.

74

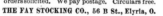

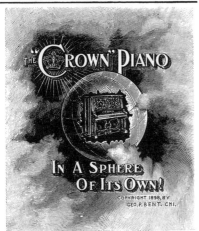

1899

THIS BOOKLET, brief and to the point, tells about a matter of which nearly every intelligent person has heard a little. Many persons who would naturally be greatly interested, if they knew more, on account of their pocket books and comfort, have not heard the real facts about the latest and best artificial light—**Acetylene.**

The real facts, as impartially set forth in this little booklet, may satisfy you, if you have a dwelling in the country, are interested in a church, institution or factory, or wish to procure the very best and cheapest artificial light for any purpose outside of a large city, that Acetylene Gas is what you have always been looking for.

This booklet sent to any address free of charge.

<table>
<tr><td>45 Broadway
NEW YORK</td><td>Union Carbide Company</td><td>157 Michigan Ave.
CHICAGO.</td></tr>
</table>

Spaulding & Co.,

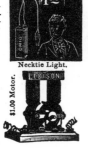

85

Domestic Water Supply.

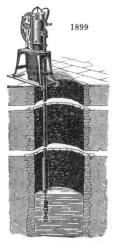

1899

AS we are frequently asked whether our Rider and Ericsson Hot Air Pumps are arranged for pumping from deep wells (both open wells and artesian), we show here the engines arranged for doing this kind of work. The Rider and the Ericsson Hot Air Pumps are as well adapted for deep well work as when used for pumping from cisterns, rivers or springs.

For further information

send for catalogue G to the nearest store. Call and see engines in operation.

RIDER-ERICSSON ENGINE CO.

22 Cortlandt St., New York.   86 Lake St., Chicago.   239 Franklin St., Boston.
    40 North 7th St., Philadelphia.   692 Craig St., Montreal, P. Q.
22A Pitt St., Sydney, N. S. W.   Teniente-Rey 71, Havana, Cuba.

CAMERAS AT LOWER PRICES

Send 50c and we will ship by express for your inspection any one of these cameras. If you like them on examination, pay the express agent express charges and balance as follows : $10.75 for Yale Model "A"; $6.95 for Yale Cycle Camera; $2.75 for Yale Model; and 95c. for Yale Jr. Write to-day.

YALE MODEL A.

$11.25 BUYS $22.00 YALE CAMERA 1899
QUANTITY LIMITED AT THIS PRICE.

Yale Model "A" takes 4 x 5 inch pictures. Most compact camera made. Highly polished seasoned mahogany throughout. All fittings nickel-plated and perfectly adjusted. Covered with highest grade black grain leather. Has rich red leather bellows, is fitted with extra rapid rectilinear lens, the best lens for general work, mounted in pneumatic release shutter, adjustable for time, instantaneous and bulb exposures. Has rising and falling front and roll holder attachment to substitute for plates. Swing back is easily operated and held firmly in any required position. Sole leather carrying case with shoulder strap and one double plate-holder go free with camera. Write to-day.

$7.45 BUYS A $15.00 CYCLE CAMERA

Yale 4 x 5 Cycle Camera comes in sole leather case with shoulder strap. Made of polished mahogany, nickel-plated trimmings, covered with extra grade grain leather. Double lens, bulb release, heavy bellows, adjustable view finder, tripod sockets and one double plate-holder. This camera was never offered by anyone for less than $15.00. Write to-day.

YALE JR.

$3.25 BUYS $5.00 YALE MODEL CAMERA

Here is a special offer of $3.25 on our Yale Model $5.00 Camera. Takes pictures 4 x 5 inches. Well made of seasoned hardwood, covered with best quality leather; two tripod sockets, two view finders, time and snap shot shutter with movable diaphragms. Will hold six plates in three double plate-holders. A double plate-holder free with each camera. This is better than many $5.00 cameras, and costs you only $3.25. Write to-day.

YALE MODEL.

$1.45 BUYS $2.50 YALE JR. CAMERA

Another offer never before made by anyone. Our $2.50 Yale Jr. at $1.45. Takes pictures 2½ x 2½ inches. Made of well seasoned wood, covered with best grade leather, single achromatic lens and view finder, time and snap shot shutter, with rotating diaphragm, and carries six plates in three double plate-holders. A double plate-holder free with each camera. Write to-day.

Write for Catalogue of Bargains in Cameras and Supplies.

YALE CAMERA CO., 37 Randolph Street, Chicago

*There is no Kodak but the
Eastman Kodak.*

1899

Photographic Simplicity

reaches the highest stage of development in the

Bulls-Eye Kodak

Daylight loading with non-breakable film cartridges, the finest fixed focus achromatic lenses, simple rotary shutters that are always set, ready for use—these are features of the No. 2 Bulls-Eye Kodaks. They are fitted with sockets for tripod screws, have large finders, are covered with the finest seal grain leather and have handsomely nickeled fittings. They are neat in appearance, convenient in use and are RELIABLE—THEY WORK. Size of picture, 3½ x 3½ inches.

PRICE.

No. 2 Bulls-Eye Kodak, for 3½ x 3½ pictures, - - - - - - - -	$8.00
Light Proof Film Cartridge, 12 exposures, - - - - - - - -	.60
Bulls-Eye Developing and Printing Outfit, - - - - - - - -	1.00

Kodaks, $5.00 to $35.00.

*Catalogues free at the dealers
or by mail.*

EASTMAN KODAK CO.
Rochester, N. Y.

Improved CYCLONE Magazine

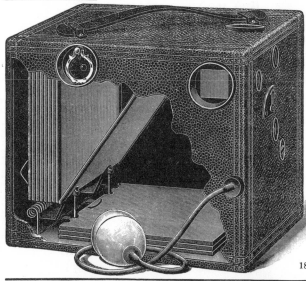

HAS { Bulb Shutter
Diaphragms
Aluminum Holders
Register
Two Finders
Quick Lens

IS { Smaller
Lighter
Neater
More
Positive } Than any
other Plate
Camera
made

No. 4, Size 3¼ x 4¼, $8.00
No. 5, Size 4 x 5, $10.00

Live Dealers Sell Them
CATALOGUE
FREE

Western Camera Mfg. Co.

1899   137 Wabash Avenue
CHICAGO

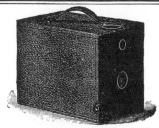

VIVES

Lead Everywhere.

"MY PAPA OWNS A VIVE."

Taken with a 4¼ x 4¼ Tourist Daylight-Loading Vive, SHOWING VALUE OF FOCUSING ATTACHMENT.

THREE DISTINCT LINES OF VIVES

IN MANY STYLES AND SIZES, WITH **IRIS DIAPHRAGMS.** 1899

1st. **Daylight-Loading Tourist Vives,** for either *Cartridge Roll Films, Glass Plates, or Cut Films*, for any number of exposures without having to go to a dark room to change,

$5.00 to $15.00

2d. **M P C Vives,** or our new **Mechanical** (12 glass) **Plate Changing** Cameras, having **all** and more advantages than other makes of this class including **Pneumatic Bulb Release,**

$6.00 to $11.50

3d. Our 1899 **Line of Highly Finished Mahogany Folding Vives,** fitted with the celebrated combined pneumatic bulb lever and time release Unicum Shutters,

$9.00 to $75.00

Style C. **M P C**

...ALL CAMERAS FULLY GUARANTEED...

Space will not permit elucidating further, but before buying a camera, send for our FREE 1899 Art Catalogue and Vive Brochure, or 5 cents for a finely Embossed mounted Sample Photograph.

VIVE CAMERA COMPANY (Manufacturers of Cameras and Photo Supplies)

Home Office: Northwest Corner State and Washington Sts., Chicago, U. S. A.

London Office: Regent House, Regent St., W.

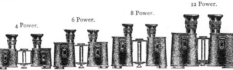

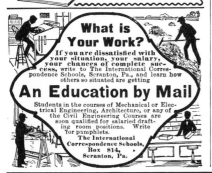

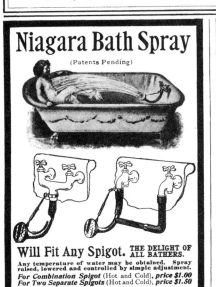

97

Jenkinson's Stogies

The tastes of smokers vary, but there is a Jenkinson Stogie for every taste. They are made of Pennsylvania and Connecticut leaf as well as of clear Havana. They are made mild, medium and strong, and are sorted and graded just as cigars are. The factory where they are made is one of the sights of Pittsburg. It is always open to the public. It is a 7-story building, light and airy, and of perfect sanitary conditions. The highest class of labor is employed—our men are paid more than cigar-makers are. It ought to be worth something to the smoker to know that his smokes are made in a factory as clean as his own parlor—and by people he wouldn't hesitate to welcome there—instead of in some foul, dingy cellar, in contact with filth and disease. In Pittsburg you will see everybody—from the workingman to the millionaire—smoking our stogies. That's because they know where and how they are made, and how good they are.

We want you to get acquainted with their merits. Ask your dealer for them. If he doesn't carry them we'll send you for $1.50 a box of 100 of our "Standard Hand-Mades" with the understanding that your money is to be refunded if, after smoking ten, you say you want it.

THE R. & W. JENKINSON CO.,
1159 Liberty Street,   Pittsburg, Pa.

A Box of 100

for $1.50

Express

1899

Prepaid

GOLF RASH

HEAT RASH, or any irritation produced by athletics or exposure, prickly heat, sunburn, tan, bites and stings of insects, inflammations, itching, irritation, and chafings, undue or offensive perspiration, and for many sanative uses, there is nothing so cooling, so purifying, and so refreshing as a bath with

Cuticura SOAP

the most effective skin purifying and beautifying soap in the world, followed when necessary by gentle anointings with CUTICURA, the great skin cure and purest of emollients.

Sold throughout the world. POTTER DRUG AND CHEM. CORP., Sole Props., Boston. Send for " How to Preserve the Skin in Summer," free.

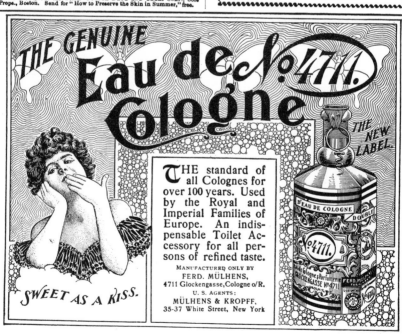

THE GENUINE Eau de Cologne No. 4711.

THE NEW LABEL.

THE standard of all Colognes for over 100 years. Used by the Royal and Imperial Families of Europe. An indispensable Toilet Accessory for all persons of refined taste.

MANUFACTURED ONLY BY
FERD. MÜLHENS,
4711 Glockengasse, Cologne o/R.
U. S. AGENTS:
MÜLHENS & KROPFF,
35-37 White Street, New York

SWEET AS A KISS.

104

105

106

LOST 40 lbs.
OF FAT.

Are You Too Stout ?

If so, why not reduce your weight and be comfortable? Obesity predisposes to Heart Trouble, Paralysis, Liver Diseases, Constipation, Rheumatism, Apoplexy, etc., and is not only dangerous but extremely annoying to people of refined taste. We do not care how many REDUCTION remedies you may have taken without success, we have a treatment that will reduce weight, as thousands can testify. The following are a few who have been reduced in weight and greatly improved in health by its use:

Mrs. C. Bliss, 59 Hudson B'k, Rochester, N. Y., reduced **20** lbs.
Mrs. Laura L. Martin, Buck Creek, Ind., reduced **65** lbs.
Mrs. M. M. Cummins, Ottawa, Ill., reduced **78** lbs.
Miss M. Hoisington, Lake View, Mich., reduced **50** lbs.
Mr. W. A. Pollock, Hartington, Neb., reduced **50** lbs.

Mrs. Helen Weber of Marietta, O., says: "It reduced my weight 40 lbs. without sickness or any inconvenience whatever."

We are going to give away barrels and

BARRELS of Sample Boxes Free.

1899

just to prove how effective, pleasant and safe this remedy is, to reduce weight. If you want one, send us your name and address and 4 cents to cover postage. Each box is mailed in a plain sealed package with no advertising on it to indicate what it contains. Price, large size box, $1.00, postpaid. Correspondence strictly confidential.

HALL CHEMICAL CO.,
N. E. Box, St. Louis, Mo.

THE MAN OF THE HOUR.

The Remarkable Achievements of Prof. Weltmer, the Great Healer, Are Causing Universal Astonishment.

The Nineteenth Century has been correctly termed the most important in scientific advancement and mental development, but no new discovery in any line is at this time attracting such widespread attention as Prof. Weltmer's Method of Magnetic Healing. In fact, the phenomenal cures made by him during the past two years have been so remarkably astounding and wonderful as to demand the attention of scientific and medical men all over the world. His method of treatment banishes disease as if by magic. Hon. Press Irons, Mayor of Nevada, was afflicted with kidney trouble for ten years and could find no relief in the usual remedies. In one week he was completely restored by Prof. Weltmer. Not only does this remarkable man cure hundreds in his Infirmary, but he possesses the ability to cure at a distance, and all cures made by this method are equally permanent. Mrs. Jennie L.

PROF. WELTMER.

Linch, Lakeview, Mo., was for two years afflicted with heart and stomach troubles. In less than 30 days she was cured. Mrs. M. M. Walker, Poca, W. Va., suffered severely with eczema, and was entirely restored by Prof. Weltmer in a month. Thousands of other sufferers all over the land have been restored in the same manner. Send for a copy of the Magnetic Journal, a 40-page illustrated magazine, giving a long list of the most astounding cures ever performed. It is sent free.

TEACHES HIS ART TO OTHERS. Prof. Weltmer teaches his wonderful art to others, and it is the grandest and best paying profession of the age. Many of his students are making $10.00 to $50.00 per day. Taught by mail or personal instructions.

Address, Prof. S. A. Weltmer, Nevada, Mo., The American School of Magnetic Healing.

Tells its ···· Own Story

TRADE RUBIFOAM MARK

RUBIFOAM
A DELIGHTFULLY FRAGRANT
LIQUID DENTIFRICE
∴∴ FOR THE TEETH
KEEPS THE TEETH WHITE, THE BREATH SWEET AND THE GUMS HEALTHY
CONTAINS NO GRIT NO ACID NOR ANYTHING INJURIOUS
∴∴ DIRECTIONS
DIP THE BRUSH IN WATER SPRINKLE ON A FEW DROPS OF RUBIFOAM AND APPLY IN THE USUAL MANNER

PRICE 25¢ A BOTTLE
PUT UP BY
E. W. HOYT & CO.,
PROPRIETORS OF
HOYT'S GERMAN COLOGNE
LOWELL MASS

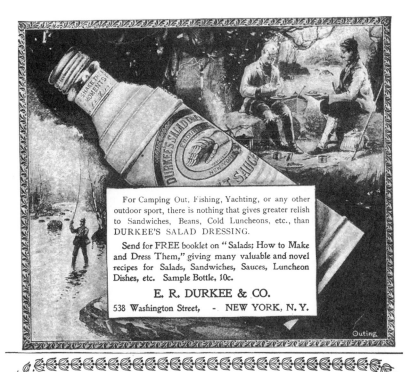
111

The Benedict "
Little Cigar
One Hundred—One Dollar

1899
The Benedict
100 for $1.00

The short smoke is the popular smoke of the day.

The BENEDICT little cigar is very decidedly the best of all short smokes.

It was brought out after a most careful study of all kinds of cigars and of the reasons for their various degrees of popularity.

And it has made a hit—a big hit.

It is the product of a large, clean, perfectly equipped factory.

It has a strictly clear Havana filler.

It is three and three-fourths inches long.

It is a perfectly made cigar and, although considerably smaller than an ordinary cigar, it affords as long a smoke as most men care for.

One hundred, in a handsome wooden box, for one dollar—and your money back if you do not like them.

Send the dollar to-day.

BENEDICT & COMPANY
321 East First Street   -   -   -   DAYTON, OHIO

REFERENCE: The Third, The Fourth, and the City National Bank of Dayton.

CHARLES AUSTIN BATES N Y

The Summer Morning Breakfast.

Pillsbury's VITOS, the ideal wheat food, does not heat the blood. It is sterilized, and will keep until used. Fruit, Pillsbury's VITOS with cream, and tea or coffee, form an admirable menu for a summer morning breakfast. Pillsbury's VITOS, being made from hard spring wheat grown in the famous Red River Valley of the North, contains an unusual percentage of gluten, and feeds both body and brain. It is natural nourishment for summer. Write for book of VITOS recipes.

THE PILLSBURY-WASHBURN FLOUR MILLS CO., Ltd., MINNEAPOLIS, MINN.
GROCERS EVERYWHERE SELL VITOS.

Pettijohn's Breakfast Food

THE WHOLE OF THE WHEAT

Nurses Recommend It.

The happiness which springs from perfect health is alone ample reason why you should eat little meat in summer, and **Pettijohn's Breakfast Food**, which contains all the elements of nutrition, affords an easy, perfectly satisfactory and delicious substitute for meat. All of the wheat but the overcoat.

At all Grocers, in 2-lb. Packages.

Most girls have some dainty belongings that they delight in caring for themselves, and by this careful attention they preserve the beauty of their pretty things and avoid the destructive tendencies of a careless laundress.

The main thing needed in washing delicate fabrics is a perfectly safe soap. Ivory Soap has been shown by the most critical tests to be made of only pure materials. Ivory Soap is effective, yet so mild that it is safe to use on anything that water will not injure.

1899

IVORY SOAP IS 99 $\frac{44}{100}$ PER CENT. PURE.

Old Prob.
Senior

1899

There is an older old probability than the Signal Service Chief. The original is a twin of human life.

Probability pervades all business affairs. To reckon with it well is to succeed; to ignore it is to fail; to wait till it is entirely eliminated is not to start.

In Newspaper Advertising the element of probability is naturally a specially interesting factor. In this line it is like the sweet potato in Aunt Dinah's famous pies—the less of that the better.

The best forecasters as to probability are observation and experience. These are what the Weather Bureau works with, and these are what we place at the service of Newspaper and Magazine Advertisers.

If any one is interested in the probability of such a plan in such papers producing such a result with such an outlay, he might find a good answer in our wide experience of thirty years. It's wise to be as wise as possible before the event.

An inquiry need cost nothing. If you are interested in Newspaper Advertising, we are interested in you.

N. W. AYER & SON,
PHILADELPHIA.

NEWSPAPER ADVERTISING.

MAGAZINE ADVERTISING.

PHOTOGRAPH OF STANLEY AUTOMOBILE STANDARD CARRIAGE NO. I.
This Carriage is now being manufactured by   1899

THE AUTOMOBILE COMPANY OF AMERICA.

Amzi Lorenzo Barber, President.   John Brisben Walker, Vice-President.
Freeland O. Stanley and Francis E. Stanley, General Managers.

THE placing of the Stanley Horseless Carriage on the market—the Stanley factory is now turning out more than ten carriages per day—opens up a new era. It brings within the reach of the man of ordinary means the power to travel in his own conveyance, at a rate of speed up to forty miles an hour—a rate of speed limited only by the character of the road—at a cost that is almost nominal.

It is possible, with the Stanley Carriage—the purchase price involves an outlay of but $600—to live twenty miles out of the city, and to make the daily trip in and out for a charge not exceeding three cents per passenger either way.

The results attained by the horseless carriage have been so startling that they are not at first understood by the public. It is scarcely saying too much to predict that the automobile carriage is destined to revolutionize methods of living and methods of travel.

The claim made for the Stanley Standard Carriage No. 1 is that it has no equal on the world's markets.

FIRST. A Demonstrated Success.	It is a demonstrated success. A single carriage has been tested over runs aggregating ten thousand miles, without appreciable injury. The movement of the machine, and its workmanlike construction, have attracted the widest admiration wherever shown.
SECOND. Regarding the Price—$600.	Although of the highest class of workmanship in every particular, no motor carriage has ever been placed on the market at so low a price. Six hundred dollars (f. o. b) for a carriage ready to take the road, places it within the reach of every class.
THIRD. Lightness of Construction.	The weight of this carriage is less than four hundred pounds, including its entire machinery, water tanks, etc. Fuel sufficient to carry it one hundred miles, adds but twenty-three pounds to this weight. It has capacity for water storage sufficient for a forty-mile run on ordinary roads, and may be refilled at any watering-trough as easily as a horse can be watered.

@ @ MOTOR VEHICLES 𝒟 𝒟

FOURTH. Is It Safe?	IN REGARD TO BOILER CONSTRUCTION. These boilers have an estimated strength of three thousand pounds to the square inch. They are tested up to one thousand pounds to the square inch. The actual steam pressure carried is but one hundred and fifty pounds to the square inch. It is believed that they are absolutely

safe for four reasons : First. The pressure used is but a fraction of the strength. Second. The fuel supply is cut off automatically when the pressure reaches one hundred and fifty pounds. Third. There is on the boiler a safety valve, which operates at one hundred and seventy pounds. Fourth. If the water supply should be exhausted in the boiler through oversight, the pressure would cease, as the boilers cease to produce steam, and with the decreased pressure of steam, the carriage would come to a stop and the pumps which supply water cease to work.

FIFTH. Automatic Devices for Regulation and Safety.	The carriage can stand for an hour while the owner is making a call. He has upon his return but to put his hand on the lever and move off at full speed, the fuel and steam being turned off and on automatically.

SIXTH. Has Climbed a 36 per cent. Grade.	The requisite of being able to climb the steepest road grades is one of the most important. To be stalled on a steep hill road would involve endless annoyance. The Stanley Carriage can climb a fourteen per cent. grade, which is considered to be a pretty steep country road grade, at fifteen miles per hour.

SEVENTH. Exhilaration of Rapid Motion.	The delight which comes of rapid movement has never been understood until one occupies a place in a horseless carriage on a smooth road. There is an exhilaration from the swift motion surpassing that of any other form of movement. The Stanley Carriage is capable of a speed of from thirty to forty-two miles per hour, according to the gear used, and racers are made to exceed even this.

EIGHTH. Made Ready in Three Minutes.	The Stanley Horseless Carriage may be gotten ready by an expert in three minutes. In common use it requires from five to ten minutes to get up its fullest power.

1899

NINTH. Two Persons Carried 72 Miles at a Cost of 17½c.	In every country drug store is sold the oil from which the machine generates its fuel gas. Seven cents a gallon is the ordinary price. Two and a half gallons carried the Stanley Carriage seventy-two miles at a recent test—total cost seventeen and one-half cents—a cost of less than a quarter of a cent per mile for two persons and less than one-eighth cent per mile for each person.

TENTH.	The machinery is of a character which can be repaired easily and inexpensively at any machine-shop in any part of the country.

ELEVENTH. Comfort.	The Stanley Carriage is operated without jolt, or jar, or vibration of any kind.

TWELFTH. Almost Noiseless.	When running along a level or nearly level road, the machinery makes absolutely no noise. When climbing a grade, a slight puffing is audible, but nothing in the least degree objectionable.

THIRTEENTH. Art of Operating Easily Mastered.	The art of operating the Stanley Carriage is easily and quickly mastered by a man or woman of fair intelligence ; and a few hours' instruction for a couple of days will give a full comprehension of the carriage and its operation in every particular. Not the twentieth part of the knowledge required for the handling and caring for a horse is required for the horseless carriage.

FOURTEENTH. Supply of Fuel.	The carriage carries a supply of fuel capable of driving the carriage one hundred miles over a good road. Water must be supplied at intervals of about forty miles.

FIFTEENTH. Light, Graceful Appearance.	The question of the light and graceful appearance of the Stanley Motor Carriage is best answered by the photographic reproduction here given.

TO SUM UP:

The Stanley Carriage costs but six hundred dollars.
It weighs less than 400 pounds.
It has a record of ten thousand miles' use without appreciable wear.
It has a record of seventy-two miles at a cost of seventeen and a half cents for fuel.
It carries fuel for one hundred miles.
It is simple in construction, odorless when running, and almost noiseless.

It can speed at any gait up to forty miles per hour or follow the slowest truck.
It is operated by steam, the standard power of the world, under perfect regulation and test.
It can be made ready to run in five minutes—in fact, the perfect piece of machinery and the only perfect automobile now on the market.

For further particulars address

THE AUTOMOBILE COMPANY OF AMERICA,

NEW YORK OFFICES : { No. 11 BROADWAY, 16TH FLOOR.
180 TIMES B'LD'G, 10TH FLOOR.   FACTORY,
NEW ENGLAND OFFICE : } NEWTON, MASS.

1899

TOBACCO

Old English CURVE CUT

is natural pipe tobacco, and is free from flavoring, coloring, and anything artificial. It is cut in slices, just right to fill the average size pipe, and for this reason there is no waste and loss every time you fill your pipe, as there is with all other kinds of pipe tobacco.

Send Ten Cents

1899

in stamps, just as soon as you can, for a trial box of this new pipe tobacco. You will enjoy the tobacco and you will like the curved box. It is a brand new idea for all "out-door" pipe smokers.

It fits the pocket.

"A slice to a pipeful."

This is the new curved box.

A SLICE TO A PIPEFUL
CONVENIENT
CHOICE QUALITY
Old English CURVE CUT Pipe Tobacco
IT FITS THE POCKET

The New Curved Box is the most convenient pocket box for pipe tobacco ever made. It is a new idea, and a good one. Every Golf player, Yachtsman, Bicyclist, Canoeist, Camper, Fisherman, and "out-door" pipe smoker will instantly recognize its practical desirability.

This Tobacco satisfies experienced pipe smokers, and is surprisingly acceptable to beginners, because it is really mellow and "cool" when smoked.

If you only knew how perfect is this combination of proper pipe tobacco and "just right" box, *you would not be without it this summer.*

You can know in a few days, if you will send us ten cents in stamps, with your name and address, as we will send you a full size box by return mail, and with it we will send an interesting and very practical illustrated talk about pipe smoking that will help you get more solid comfort out of your pipe.

Address Sales Depart. R. The American Tobacco Company, 111 Fifth Avenue, New-York City.

TOBACCO

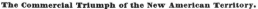

The Commercial Triumph of the New American Territory.

The Advanced New Era Standard of Excellence in Cigar-leaf, hand-made, "Lucke" Style.
Investigate !
This is worth *knowing* about.
The smoker who remains ignorant of what this product is, cheats himself of both money and satisfaction.

THE LUCKE
ROLLED CIGAR
BOX OF 50 | Sent to any Address in U. S., Express paid by us for . . . . | $1.25

BOX OF 100, ... $2.25.

LONG FILLER ### A PERFECT FULL SMOKE **LONG FILLER**

A free-draft quick roll of the finest filler stock now obtainable in the world.
This stock is a choice selection from the loam soil, new growth Porto Rican crops, for gaining the control of which our firm excited so much comment last fall.   Experts pronounce it fully the equal of the finest Cuban Vuelta crops of former days.   Wholly of a different class from coarse, flavorless and unclimatic domestic tobacos which are entirely unsuited for cigars.   A relief also from the inferior Havana stock this country has been getting from Cuba for some time past.
Send for a box and smoke a few. If to your taste they're not eloquent arguments for "colonial" develop-ment—if not equal in flavor, draft and true satisfying qualities, (hundreds of clubmen and smokers of fine cigars write us that in flavor these goods are far superior) to any 2 for 25c. or 3 for 50c. cigar you can buy today—your money is on call—we will return same at once.

WE ALSO OFFER
A REVELATION TO THE AMERICAN SMOKER IN

1899

LUCKES' ROLLS
BOX OF 100 | Prepaid to any ad-dress in U. S. for | $1.00

Four inches in length, made of stock from same crops as the Lucke Rolled Cigar, which is revolutionizing American cigar trade.

The common small cigar made from "scrap" stock,—the offal of cigar factories and, latterly of course, leavings from a cigar stock that is the worst that ever prevailed in the United States,— have created a natural prejudice against the small cigar.
"Lucke's Rolls" are not made from scrap of any kind.
"Lucke's Rolls" have a **Long Filler.**
It is the **best flavored** long filler obtainable to-day.
"Lucke's Rolls" are made of three layers of fine, clean leaf rolled up in a wrapper.
"Lucke's Rolls" are not merely the **best short smoke.**   They are a small cigar, every whiff of which is a pleasure to the tobacco connoiseur.

IF YOU DON'T FIND IT SO
—we present you with the number of smokes it takes to find it out, and
WE REFUND ALL YOUR MONEY.
No expense to you, no arguments and no delay about it.   Remit price of goods only, we prepay delivery.

J. H. LUCKE & CO., | ADDRESS SAMPLE SALES DEPT., LUCKE BLOCK, | CINCINNATI, OHIO.

Most Extensive Manufacturers in the World of Fine Special Goods

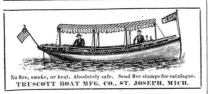

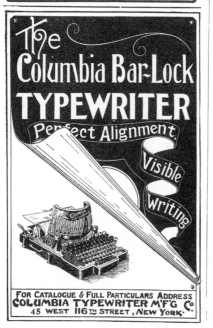

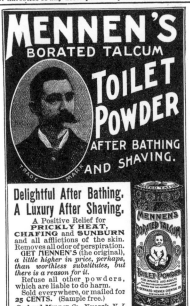

131

132

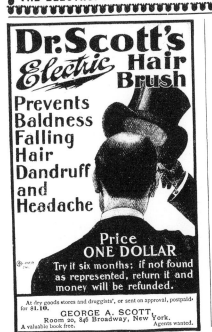

133

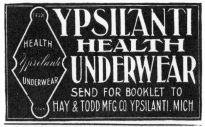

Wearers of ....

QUEEN QUALITY
Shoes

Will find it to their advantage to use

1899

QUEEN QUALITY DRESSING

Which can be obtained wherever Queen Quality Shoes are sold.

The use of this dressing insures a longer life for the shoe than when any other is used. The finest oils and other necessary ingredients are carefully selected with a view to preserving the leather.

Queen Quality Shoes are sold by only **one dealer** in a town. One price. **$3**

(Oxfords $2.50.)

Illustrated Catalogue

Showing styles for street, dress, house or outing wear, sent **FREE** with **address of local dealer.**

Shoes sent prepaid on receipt of price and 25 cts. extra for express or mail charges.

THOS. G. PLANT CO., 1 BICKFORD ST., BOSTON, MASS.

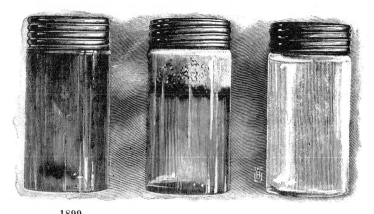

1899

Result:

Above are samples of "Soft Soap" or "Soap Paste" made with PEARLINE, and with two of the *leading* powders which are claimed to be "Same as" or "Good as" PEARLINE.

The bottle to the right contains a solid mass of pure, white "Soap Paste" or "Soft Soap," made with PEARLINE—thick enough to stand alone.

The bottle in the middle is one of "Same as," and contents is one-quarter poor, thin, mushy soap—balance (three-quarters) discolored water.

The bottle to the left is a poorer "Same as," and contains simply discolored water, with a sediment (not soapy) at bottom. The middle and left-hand bottles are fair samples of the many powders offered in place of PEARLINE. Try the experiment yourself—directions on back of each package.

Some powders are worthless, some inefficient, others dangerous. *Pearline is the standard.* The Millions of Packages of PEARLINE used each year proves

Pearline Best by Test

Note.

The difference in price between **Pearline** and the most worthless Soap Powders is nominal. A year's supply would not equal the value of one ordinary garment ruined.

Hay Fever and Asthma
Cured to Stay Cured. 1899

Why not Consult
Dr. P. Harold Hayes,
Buffalo, N. Y., as to
your Hay-Fever or
Asthma?

He has treated forty
Thousand Cases and can
do more for you than
any other physician

It costs nothing for
his opinion as to your
curability and he will
frankly advise for your
best interests.

Why Suffer _needlessly_?

References to cured patients in all parts of the world.   Full information
with Examination paper and Thesis free on application.

Address P. HAROLD HAYES, M. D., Buffalo, N. Y.

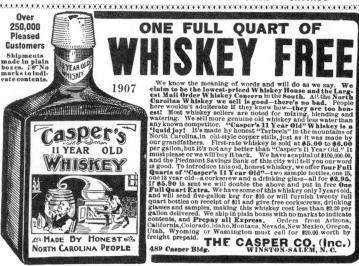

NOTE:

All ads appearing in this Scrapbook are of course void. They are reproduced not for the purpose of selling any merchandise, but for their historical interest. They afford an interesting comparison of the advertising methods of today and those in use earlier in the century.

WINCHESTER

REPEATING RIFLES AND SHOTGUNS

TEN DIFFERENT MODELS—
ALL DESIRABLE CALIBERS, STYLES AND WEIGHTS.

GUNS FOR ALL KINDS OF SHOOTING AND AMMUNITION FOR ALL KINDS OF GUNS·

FREE *Send name and Address on a postal for 156 Page Illustrated Catalogue.*

WINCHESTER REPEATING ARMS CO. NEW HAVEN, CONN.

1899

FROM CLEVELAND TO NEW YORK.

A Winton Motor Phaeton

Made the run from Cleveland to New York City May 22nd to 26th.

Distance Traveled, 707.4 Miles.
Actual Running Time, 47 hrs. and 34 min.
Average Speed per hour 15½ Miles.

A convincing demonstration and a record that will stand. Hydro-Carbon System.

Write us for particulars.

THE WINTON MOTOR CARRIAGE CO.,
472-478 Belden St.,   Cleveland, Ohio.

Baker's Bedside Table.

Adjustable for serving meals or for reading, writing, etc. Does not touch the bed. IN FOUR STYLES: Black enameled, $4; white enameled, $4.50; nickel-plated, $6.50; antique copper-plated (very handsome), $7. FREIGHT PREPAID east of Mo. River and north of North Carolina. W. W. Godding, M.D., Supt. Government Hospital at Washington, D.C., writes: " Please ship us four dozen White Enameled Bedside Tables. They are the best invalid bedside tables we have found, and we have tried several kinds."

Interesting booklet mailed free. Be sure to send for it.
J. R. BAKER & SONS CO.,
33 Wayne St., Kendallville, Ind.

139

Save your horse

Slipping impossible, no matter how smooth the pavement.

No more calks and pads to injure hoofs, lame the horse, and change his gait.

Perfect tread with absolute safety and comfort.

Confidence and freedom of action humanely restored to every horse shod with the

"ROUGH RIDER"

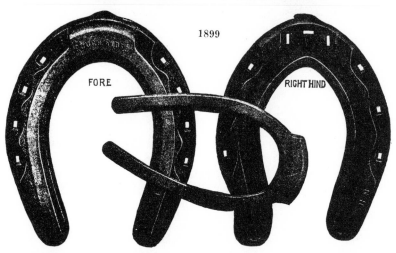

A STEEL SHOE DROP-FORGED, with EXPANDING RUBBER TREAD, maintaining until worn out a **constant rubber contact** with the pavement by the expansion of the rubber within a dovetailed groove, **absolutely preventing slipping** and giving a perfectly natural tread. Can be forged to fit, hot or cold, and rubber securely inserted before fastening to the hoof. It is not an experiment. It is the result of three years of actual use, demonstrating a PERFECT HORSESHOE. **Invaluable on smooth and slippery pavements.** Regard your own safety. Try it on your favorite horse; he will feel and be a better animal.

If your blacksmith hasn't the "ROUGH RIDER" SHOE, send us his name and address and we will see that he gets them for you. Write to us for a pamphlet giving information and facts that will convince the most skeptical.

Don't forget that we will send you **free** upon application our valuable and interesting pamphlet, including reproductions of **testimonials of the very highest** order, embracing **recommendations** of the **most noted horsemen** in the country.

EXPANDING TREAD CO., 149 Broadway, New York

The Carpenter Electric Vehicle.

—o—

H. H. Carpenter, of Denver, Col., presents an electric vehicle of unusually light and pleasing construction, in which a storage battery of his own invention is used. The front wheels are of bicycle build, and the steering is operated by a lever.

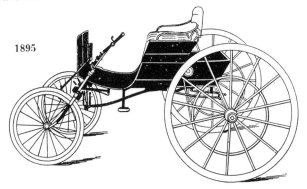

1895

ELECTRIC WAGON. H. H. CARPENTER, DENVER, COL.

The Elston Motor Vehicle.

—o—

R. W. Elston, of Charlevoix, Mich., enters in the *Times-Herald* Race a two-seated vehicle equipped with a Kane-Pennington engine of 4-horse power.

The steering apparatus consists of one segment, two pinions, and one steering post. Power is applied equally to both hind wheels. A speed of twenty-five miles an hour is claimed by the inventor.

1895

GASOLENE VEHICLE. R. W. ELSTON, CHARLEVOIX, MICH.

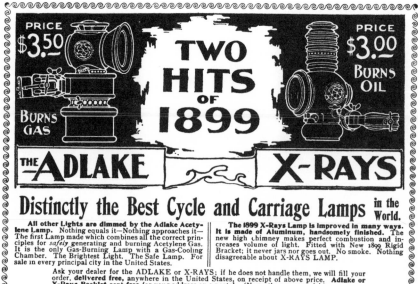

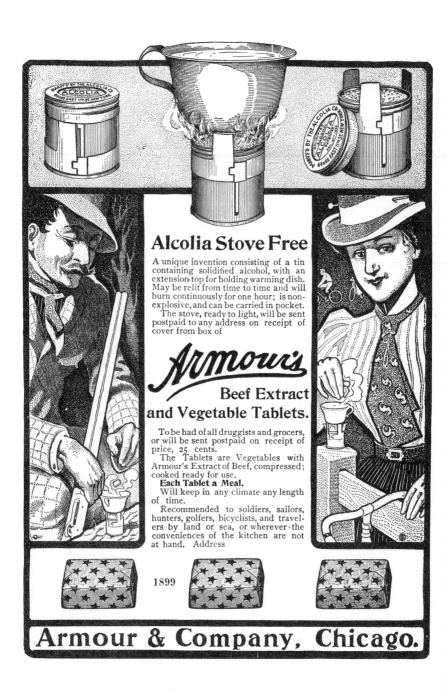

Alcolia Stove Free

A unique invention consisting of a tin containing solidified alcohol, with an extension-top for holding warming dish. May be relit from time to time and will burn continuously for one hour; is non-explosive, and can be carried in pocket.

The stove, ready to light, will be sent postpaid to any address on receipt of cover from box of

Armour's

Beef Extract
and Vegetable Tablets.

To be had of all druggists and grocers, or will be sent postpaid on receipt of price, 25 cents.

The Tablets are Vegetables with Armour's Extract of Beef, compressed; cooked ready for use.

Each Tablet a Meal.

Will keep in any climate any length of time.

Recommended to soldiers, sailors, hunters, golfers, bicyclists, and travelers by land or sea, or wherever the conveniences of the kitchen are not at hand. Address

1899

Armour & Company, Chicago.

1901

BUY A SKENE,

A successful steam automobile built by reliable makers, and enjoy the fascination of a horseless carriage. We will be pleased to demonstrate the many points of superiority which our machine possesses to any one who is interested. There is a small amount of **TREASURY STOCK** in this Company still unsubscribed. Those who are looking for a "good thing" will do well to correspond with me immediately.

ARTHUR C. EDDY, Treasurer

Skene American Automobile Company

Carr Bldg., Harrison Ave., Springfield, Mass.

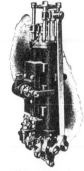

THE PHELPS TRACTOR.

—— 1901 ——

THE great advantages of the PHELPS TRACTOR lie in the fact that all the machinery is in a compact, independent form which is readily attached to any kind of a road vehicle, either for business or pleasure, and the almost complete elimination of the serious objections of heat, vibration, dirt, and smell, so annoying in gasoline motor machines.

In the construction shown herewith, the forward portion contains a small steam engine, which will deliver, with economy, any power required, from one-quarter to ten-horse power. The lower portion of the body forward of the axle contains the water tank, and back of the axle is the boiler. This is equipped with automatic fuel and water feed, and will run a half day without attention. The exhaust is muffled and condensed by passing it through the cold water tank. The driver has the TRACTOR under perfect control at all times by means of the reins only. He steers, starts, stops, reverses, and backs, regulates the speed from one to twenty miles an hour at will and with ease and certainty. Drawing in the reins slows down the speed, and finally stops and backs. Slackening the pull on the reins increases the speed, but if the reins are slackened too much, or dropped altogether, the engine stops instantly, preventing a possible runaway. All these important features are fully covered by patent allowed, which is unquestionably the most valuable patent ever allowed on motor vehicles for use on the highways.

The illustrations on this sheet represent a few of the innumerable combinations which are possible with one machine.

PHELPS TRACTOR.
(COMBINATION No. 2.)

With this combination a light supporting frame is furnished, by means of which the forward part of the carriage body is raised clear of the TRACTOR and supported there while the TRACTOR is removed. The lifting is done with a screw, and the work of changing the TRACTOR from one wagon to another can be done by one man as quickly as a horse can be similarly changed.

PHELPS TRACTOR.
(COMBINATION No. 3.)

This valuable combination added to the foregoing makes the TRACTOR of universal application. Any hired or picked-up vehicle may be quickly taken in tow. The ornamental cover to the TRACTOR is simply an open receptacle for parcels of any description. By mounting a seat on the forward part for the driver, it may be used as a small parcel delivery wagon. With a two-seated wagon in tow it makes an ideal hunting tour outfit. The tents, camp equipage and game may be carried in the TRACTOR body.

By replacing the steering wheel with a small steering runner, and exchanging the drive wheels for a pair with spikes to prevent slipping, the TRACTOR may be hitched to a sleigh and driven fast enough and far enough to satisfy the most enthusiastic, without danger of killing the horse.

For further particulars, apply to

L. J. PHELPS, New Brunswick, N. J.

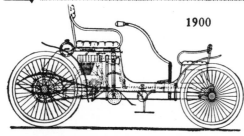
148

The Oldsmobile

Nothing to watch but the road

Used *yesterday*, in use *to-day*, and ready for *tomorrow*. The construction is simple and practical, the working parts are easily understood and readily accessible.

Power is transmitted to the rear axle by a roller chain of 4,000 pounds working strength, running direct from the motor shaft. Operated by a single lever from the seat and responds instantly to the will of the operator.

1903

This handsome and practical machine has demonstrated through every day use by 7,000 drivers its undoubted right to the title of "*The Best Thing on Wheels*."

Records

The highest awards for a perfect score in the Long Island and Chicago Endurance Runs and the New York-Boston Reliability Run. Fifteen cups for first places in speed races.

The Oldsmobile is not a racing machine, but the speed records show it can go about as fast as the average man cares to travel.

Price $650.

Write for illustrated Book to Department M.

Olds Motor Works
Detroit, Mich.

150

MANUFACTURERS, ATTENTION !

$1000 VALUE MACHINE   **Dyke's No. I Outfit**   WITH LEVERS ATTACHED TO TRANSMISSION

There is no better piece of **workmanship** or **design** on the market to-day. We have endeavored to put into our machine the **best** of everything. If you are looking for **cheap** material you will not get it in our outfit—although it will be much cheaper in the long run to get something first-class.

OUR OBJECT is to supply you with the Parts to build your machine. Although we supply you with a design of body, you can use your own taste in this selection. On the rear of the body a Tonneau can be attached and four passengers can be carried.

TANKS.—The Water and Gasoline Tank is placed in front under a Brass Hood.

ENGINE is Dyke's Single Cylinder, 5¼x6, with a No. 2 Champion Transmission built direct on the engine shaft.

THE LEVERS are arranged on a casting which is cast on the crank head of the engine. This casting also acts as outer bearing for the engine shaft.

Our outfit consists of **Dyke's No. 1 Engine, Dyke's Flexible Reachless Running Gear, Dyke's Carburetter, Dyke's Radiator, Dyke's Wheel Steering, etc.**

RUNNING GEAR is our new Model B, No. C, shown in our supplement, with **genuine** Artillery Hubs and Roller Bearings, extra heavy knuckles and finest workmanship possible. Everything guaranteed. **See testimonials** from our customers.

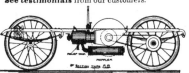

SIDE VIEW DYKE'S NO. I OUTFIT.

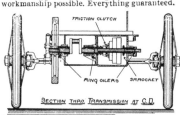

FRICTION CLUTCH

RING OILERS   SPROCKET

SECTION THRO. TRANSMISSION AT C.D.

1903

CRANK SHAFT SOLID from one end to the other. All key seats carefully milled.
2 RING OILER BEARINGS and a long bronze bearing in the center. Improved high speed friction clutch.

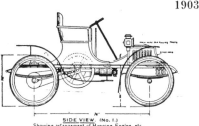

SIDE VIEW. (No. I.)
Showing arrangement of Hanging Engine, etc.

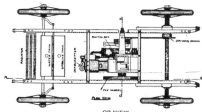

TOP VIEW.
Showing arrangement of Hanging Engines, Radiator, etc.
Attachment for holding Levers not shown.

Side View No. I Engine and Transmission.

Dyke No. I Body, with Detachable Rear Tonneau Seat and Brass Hood in Front.

FRONT AXLE,
With Genuine Artillery Hubs and Timken Roller Bearings.

Rear Axle with Roller Bearings contained in case, ready for Springs and Radius

No. 28 and No. 29,
Drop Spring Forgings.

RADIUS ROD.
Patented.

GET OUR DISCOUNT   QUANTITY ORDERS HANDLED

If purchased in sufficient quantities this entire outfit can be bought for

$485.45

Our Engine and Transmission is Sold Separately

A. L. DYKE

1402 PINE STREET   ST. LOUIS, MO.

Mr. Dyke probably originated "knock-down" or kit selling. You could buy the parts from Dyke and assemble yourself a car.—Clymer.

152

The Sholes Visible Typewriter

COMPETES WITH ANY MACHINE AT ANY PRICE, but at a retail price of $60.00   NONE CAN COMPETE WITH IT.

There are several ALLEGED VISIBLE TYPEWRITERS, in which you can see what you have written BY STOPPING AND CRANING YOUR NECK, but only ONE on which you can see what you are writing ALL THE TIME.

1903

It is the Sholes VISIBLE Typewriter.

It has fewer parts, cannot be thrown out of alignment, and is the best seller of any Typewriter made.

WRITE AT ONCE FOR AGENCY TERMS & EXCLUSIVE TERRITORY.

A. D. MEISELBACH TYPEWRITER COMPANY
KENOSHA, WIS.

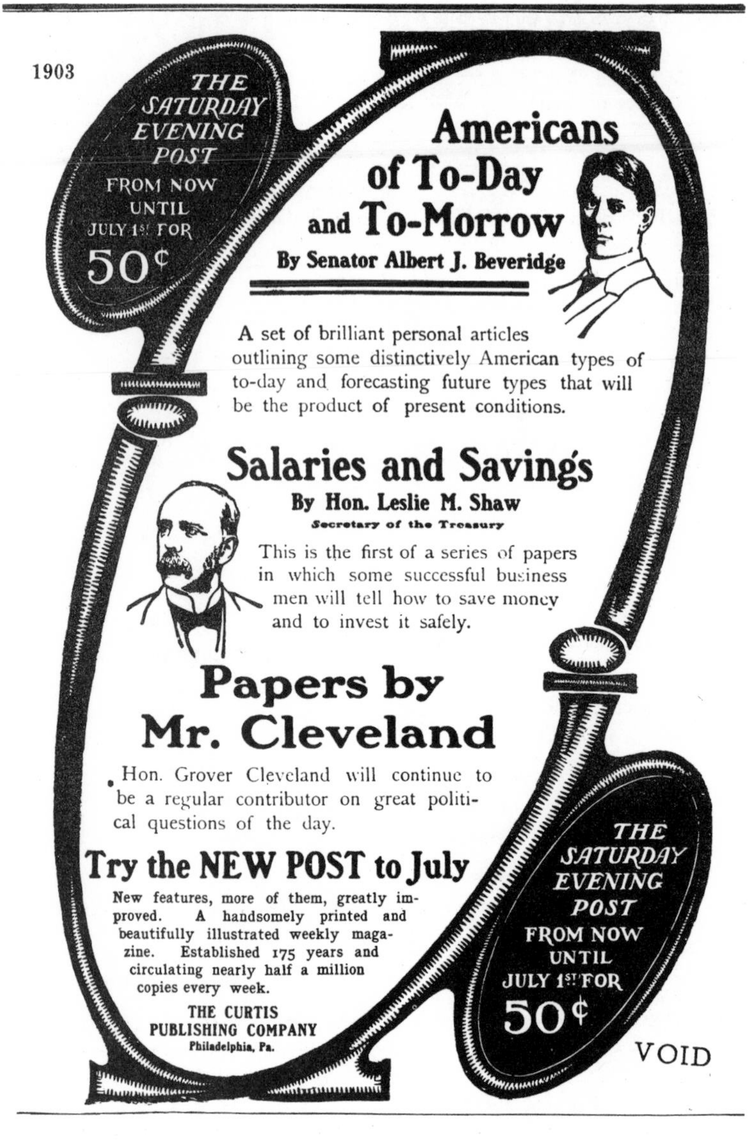

156

THE NEW GIANT ENGINE

1903

The season of 1902 was in most localities one which on account of the excessive rains tested the qualities of Engines as never before. It was hard steaming, hard threshing, hard pulling, hard on the flues, hard on the engine and hard on the engineers.

The New Giant came through the ordeal without a single failure—without a single defeat. No waiting for steam, no lack of power, no stuck in the mud; nothing but complete satisfaction of all demands made upon it.

Why ?

Because the New Giant is so constructed as to have a large reserve force to meet such conditions.

Every New Giant can develop 3 times its rated power when necessary. Our tests are recorded, so we can prove it if required.

The New Giant is the outgrowth of 30 years of successful Engine building, and contains all the improvements which during that time have been found useful. The result is an engine which for convenience, durability, economy and power is unsurpassed.

But we are talking this time mainly of power. Did you ever hear of a Giant Engine getting stuck ? On the contrary you have known plenty of instances where a 14-horse Giant did the same work as 20-horse engines of other makes. Well, the New Giant is an improved Giant, and a giant in fact as well as in name.

Look at the heavy substantial Gearing, the large Shafting, the solid construction throughout. It says Strength and Power, Power and Strength on all sides and under all conditions.

For full description see our 1903 catalogue. Drop us a card and we will put you on our mailing list, **and** that one cent for the postal card is all it will cost you.

MANUFACTURED BY THE

NORTHWEST THRESHER COMPANY

STILLWATER. MINN.

Say you saw it in The World.

157

When a Competitor Tells You

1904

that we are going to remodel our motor and increase the cylinder capacity in order to get greater power, he don't know what he's talking about. We're going to do nothing of the kind. We don't need to. We had more power in that little 5 x 5 engine of last year than was needed for ordinary work. It was tried at extraordinary work and was not found lacking. Think what it means to hook onto a load of street railway iron (seven seventy foot rails) loaded on two trucks, requiring four heavy horses to pull, the estimated weight of steel and trucks being over eight tons, and draw that load up a four per cent. grade from a standing start. A Canton (Ohio) Cadillac owner (Mr. A. H. Wilson) did it, not only once but several times. A two-cylinder opposed engine, rated at 8 horsepower, tried it and failed to move it forward an inch. Remodel the Cadillac Engine? Certainly not; there's no reason for it. When anyone tells you this

Don't You Believe Him

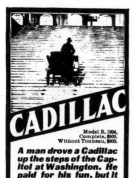

Model B, 1904,
Complete, $900.
Without Tonneau, $800.

A man drove a Cadillac up the steps of the Capitol at Washington. He paid for his fun, but it was worth the money to know the power of the Cadillac.

The Cadillac Engine of last year had ample power (it's got more this year) for those who *knew* how to operate it. A large cylinder would be no advantage to those who *do not* know how to secure all the available power a gas engine is capable of. The Cadillac Motor is, and always has been a wonder. Competitors recognized it from the first minute after it came out. Some of them have been busy "knocking" ever since; others "got wise" and made imitations; others "sawed wood;" but all are guessing. When Leland & Faulconer Manufacturing Co. makes anything, it is as near right as fine tools, gauges, dies, machinery and men assembled in a well organized and old established firm can make it. And when they tell you it has a certain horsepower, you can bank on its having more. This well known firm makes all Cadillac Motors and transmissions, and they are made well. Speaking of Transmissions reminds us—but never mind, we'll tell you about those next week; we are "all in" for want of space.

CADILLAC AUTOMOBILE COMPANY

Members of the Association of Licensed Automobile Manufacturers

DETROIT, MICH.

Independent Telephone Co.

ADVANTAGES OF A RESIDENCE TELEPHONE.

Makes engagements;
Invites your friends;
Friends can call you;
Does your shopping;
Reserves theatre tickets;
Orders your groceries;
And corrects mistakes;
Calls the plumber;

1904

Hastens the delivery of goods;
Saves letter writing;
Calls your husband;
Saves time and steps;
Runs your errands;
Calls the doctor;
Calls the fire department;
Calls the police.

In 1904 the public had to be sold on the usefulness of the telephone just like they did on the early automobile. This ad from a 1904 Seattle city directory claims some interesting reasons why a phone should be used.—Clymer.

UNCLE SAM SAYS
IT'S ALL RIGHT.

1904

Uncle Sam in the person of Ten Government Officials, has charge of every department of our distillery. During the entire process of distillation, after the whiskey is stored in barrels in our warehouses, during the seven years it remains there, from the very grain we buy to the whiskey you get, Uncle Sam is constantly on the watch to see that everything is all right. We dare not take a gallon of our own whiskey out of our own warehouse unless he says it's all right. And when he does say so, that whiskey goes direct to you, with all its original richness and flavor, carrying a **UNITED STATES REGISTERED DISTILLER'S GUARANTEE** of PURITY and AGE, and saving the dealers' big profits. That's why **HAYNER WHISKEY** is the best for medicinal purposes. That's why it is preferred for other uses. That's why we have half a million satisfied customers. That's why **YOU** should try it. Your money back if you're not satisfied.

HAYNER
WHISKEY
1 QUART $1.00
4 QUARTS $3.20

WE PAY EXPRESS CHARGES IN EITHER CASE.

Send us **$1.00** for **ONE QUART** or **$3.20** for **FOUR QUARTS of HAYNER SEVEN-YEAR-OLD RYE**, and we will pay the express charges. We ship in a plain, sealed package; no marks to even suggest contents. If you don't find it all right and better than you can buy from anybody else for double the money, ship it back to us at our expense and your money will be promptly refunded. We ship one quart on your first or trial order only. All subsequent orders must be for at least 4 quarts at 8o cents a quart. The packing and express charges are almost as much on one quart as on four and even at $1.00 for one quart we lose money, but we want you to try it. **WE PREFER TO HAVE YOU ORDER FOUR QUARTS FOR $3.20 RIGHT NOW FOR THEN WE WILL MAKE A LITTLE PROFIT AND YOU WILL ALSO SAVE MONEY.**

Trial orders for Ariz., Cal., Col., Idaho, Mont., Nev., N. Mex., Ore., Utah., Wash., or Wyo., must be 1 Quart for $1.25 by EXPRESS PREPAID. Subsequent orders on the basis of 4QUARTS for $4.00 by EXPRESS PREPAID or 20 Quarts for $16.00 by FREIGHT PREPAID.

Remit by Check, Bank Draft, Express or Money Order. It is unsafe to send currency unless you register your letter. Write our nearest office and do it **NOW.**

ESTABLISHED 1866.   **THE HAYNER DISTILLING COMPANY,**   **DISTILLERY TROY, OHIO.**

DAYTON, OHIO.   **ST. LOUIS, MO.,**   **ST. PAUL, MINN.,**   **ATLANTA, GA.,**

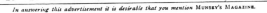

In answering this advertisement it is desirable that you mention MUNSEY'S MAGAZINE.

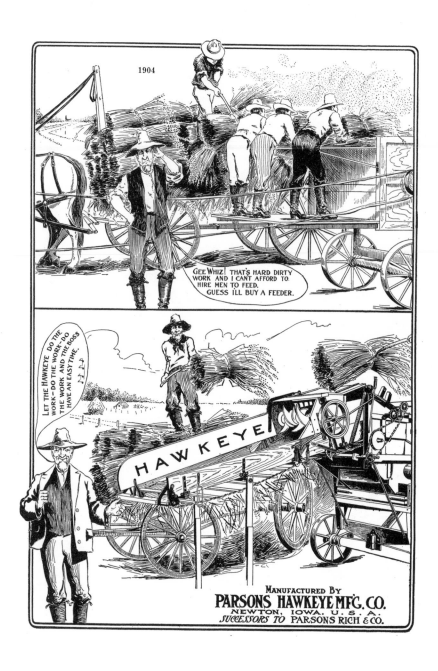

162

1905

LARKIN
PREMIUMS FREE

with **LAUNDRY and TOILET SOAPS, TOILET and PHARMACAL PREPARATIONS, COFFEE, TEAS, COCOA, EXTRACTS, BAKING POWDER, STARCHES, Etc.,** in all, nearly a hundred daily necessities.

Larkin Products have established a standard of purity and high quality—the fruition of thirty years' manufacturing experience.

With purchases of products amounting to $10.00 and up, you receive free premiums equal in value to amount paid. Larkin Premiums are the saved profits and expenses of middlemen, and are excellent in design, workmanship and finish. They furnish homes completely.

Factory=to=Family Dealing Saves Money

for over two million families annually. You get twice the value any retailer can afford to give. Thirty days' trial—satisfaction guaranteed.

WRITE FOR NEW PREMIUM LIST No. 91

Contains over 700 offers;
also ask for book of
Larkin Products.

Larkin Co.
BUFFALO, N. Y.
ESTABLISHED, 1875.

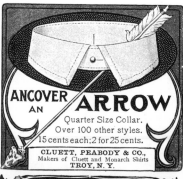

Che Watres Gas Engine Whistle

is an innovation for marine motoring. It is operated simply by spent gas and does not affect the running of the engine. Whistle blown by the touch of a cord at engineer's elbow. Blows simultaneously three tones of chromatic scale and can be clearly heard two miles away. Does away with all hand pumping. The device is simple, easily attached and has nothing to get out of order. It is absolutely safe and satisfactory. Thirty days' trial allowed, then, if not satisfactory, say so, and back goes your $35. Booklet on request.

GAS ENGINE WHISTLE COMPANY, 1137 Broadway, New York

Complete Only

$15.

BURNS WOOD or COAL

JUST SEND ME ONE DOLLAR

and I will ship C. O. D. to any railroad station in the U. S. this fine Willard Steel Range Anyone can say they have the best range in the world, but 1 will furnish the evidence and leave the verdict to you. After you examine this range, if you are satisfied in every way, pay Agent $14.00 and freight, and you become the possessor of the best range in the world for the money. The range has six 8-inch lids; 18-inch oven; 15-gallon reservoir; large warming closet; top cooking service 30x34 ins. Guaranteed to reach you in perfect order. Shipping weight, 400 lbs. Thousands in use and every one of them giving satisfaction. Write for full description and testimonials.

WM. G. WILLARD

No. 12 WILLARD BUILDING
316-320 CHESTNUT STREET   ST. LOUIS, MO

WE GUARANTEE   1905

OUR OUTFITS TO HANDLE MORE AIR FOR THE POWER CONSUMED THAN ANY OTHER SET OF THE SAME SIZE. TO BUY THEM IS GOOD **ECONOMY**. GENERATORS, VARIABLE & CONSTANT SPEED MOTORS

Rochester Electric Motor Co., 10-12 Frank Street, ROCHESTER, N. Y.

The Modern Machines for Mechanics

Here are two of the most useful and indispensable machines. The cut on the left shows the best Bench Drill ever constructed for sensitive work. Drills from smallest size up to 5-16 inch. Spindle has Morse No. 1 taper hole and is counterbalanced by coil spring around feed lever shaft. Insures perfectly true and accurate work. The Twentieth Century Polishing Lathe, see cut on right, is one of many different styles and sizes of Polishing Lathes that we manufacture. We have them to run by foot or belt power, for use in all mechanic's lines. Send for catalogues B-15, C-15.

THE W. W. OLIVER MFG. CO., 1482 Niagara St., Buffalo, N.Y.

NOTE:

All ads appearing in this Scrapbook are of course void, having appeared years ago. They are reproduced not for the purpose of selling any merchandise. The ads do, however, show the great progress made by both the automotive industry and the advertising firms of this country.

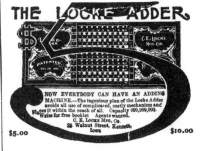

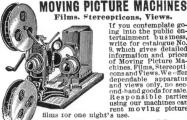

167

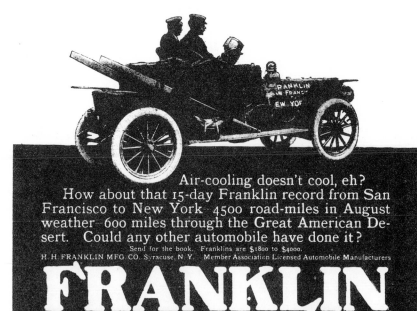

Air-cooling doesn't cool, eh? How about that 15-day Franklin record from San Francisco to New York—4500 road-miles in August weather—600 miles through the Great American Desert. Could any other automobile have done it?

Send for the book. Franklins are $1800 to $4000.
H. H. FRANKLIN MFG. CO. Syracuse, N. Y. Member Association Licensed Automobile Manufacturers

FRANKLIN

This is the same Russell E. Gardner that built the famous Gardner cars in St. Louis, Mo. The Gardner car will be illustrated in later editions of the MOTOR SCRAPBOOK.—*Clymer.*

CAN THIS BE THE FIRST DRIVE-IN? The car is a 1905 Reo. The 2-cylinder opposed engine is located under the body. Note the hand rails on the cowl, or what was then known as the dash-board. This car had the first air cleaner, as it had a screen on the carburetor air intake with a sock covering to keep out the dirt. It was chain driven. COCA-COLA, now known the world over as a famous drink, was popular, even then.—*Clymer.*

Here's a Wagon that Delights the Farmer

Because it will give years of service

IT is made of very carefully selected stock, well ironed and braced; wheels are dipped in boiling oil and round edge steel tire is used for protection of felloes and paint. **It will take much heavier loads than the average wagon with no additional horses.** This is due to the National Self-oiling Steel Tubular Axles with which it is equipped. These axles are very light running, having polished spindles and seamless ground boxes.

Mr. Dealer, if you would know the delights of a pleased patronage write us for an Acme agency. We make Farm Wagons, Contractors' Wagons and Carts. Catalogue is free.

ACME WAGON CO., Emigsville, Pa.

Salesmen, Canvassers and Implement Dealers

THE MOST COMPLETE CREAMERY OR REFRIGERATOR IN THE MONEY.

Earn Large Profits with Small Capital

Sold the Entire Year to all Classes Strictly High-Class Goods

Ask for our circulars with prices   No goods sold direct   Secure territory

ZERO CREAMERY CO. - Peru, Ind.

The LEADER GARDEN PLOW

Easy on the operator

There is no plow made that excels "The Leader" to high grade material and finish, as the entire plow, except crosshandle, is made of very best stiff steel. The attachments that go with each plow are a mould-board, with landside shovel, calf tongue, weeder and cultivator. The cultivator is better than a rake.

Patented in U. S. and Canada.

Dealers send for our catalogue and prices.

D. S. THOMAS, Manufacturer - Bridgewater, Va.

Rogers Belt Punch

Send for Circulars and Prices on the

THE neatest little article for punching holes in belts that was ever invented. In great demand by all threshermen and users of belted machinery, harness makers, farmers, etc. A hammer and block of wood are no longer needed to punch holes in belts. Punches any size hole from one-sixteenth to three-eighths inch. Retail price, 75 cents each. Sent to any address postage prepaid. If you want to sell the best little money maker you ever heard of, this is it. Write us at once. **Special prices to dealers.**

THE SATTLEY STACKER COMPANY, Indianapolis, Ind.

ECLIPSE MACHINERY

Highest Grade

ECLIPSE Traction Engine with Friction Clutch, mounted on Independent Steel Frame Work and with many special features of value. Catalog.

ECLIPSE Saw Mills, Portable Engines, Stationary Engines, Boilers, Ice and Refrigerating Machinery. Catalog.

Also the "Landis Eclipse" Separator, Wind Stackers and Attachments, Comprising the Best and Most Modern Machine Ever Offered. Catalog.

FRICK COMPANY, WAYNESBORO, PA.

COLUMBIA WAGON COMPANY

1905

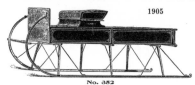

No. 382

Columbian Delivery Sleigh

We show you this week our Columbian Delivery Sleigh—just the sleigh for business or pleasure, furnished with an extra seat if desired. Write for our new catalog showing line of sleds and sleighs. Place your orders early, as our stock is limited.

COLUMBIA WAGON COMPANY, Columbia, Pa., U. S. A.

All ads appearing in this Album are, of course, void. They are not reproduced for the purpose of selling merchandise. These ads are interesting because of the changes in advertising methods over a period of years.

Over 100 different makes of electric automobiles were once manufactured in the United States. The ELECTRIC EDITION of my MOTOR SCRAPBOOK, to be published at a later date, will contain illustrations and descriptions of over 100 electrics. Two of the most popular electric cars are shown here.—Clymer.

ENTERTAIN
"The Boys" with an
Edison Phonograph
1906

THE house "the boys" like to visit is the one that's always full of good cheer—fun and music. If you want to make your home attractive, get an Edison Phonograph. It tells the funny stories of the best vaudeville monologuists. It sings the sweetest songs of the present and bygone days. It plays the latest band marches, two-steps, waltzes and quadrilles in dancing tempo. It renders perfectly the finest orchestral selections and instrumental solos. Then, too, you and your friends can have no end of fun making records at home. Truly this marvelous entertainer is unequalled. That's why it makes *the Best Holiday or Birthday Present.*

Go to the nearest Edison dealer and hear the genuine Phonograph, and you will instantly appreciate its marked superiority. The Edison signature is on every Edison Phonograph and Edison Gold Moulded Record. Phonographs, $10 up; Records, 35c. each. Send to Orange, N. J., office for new booklet, *"Home Entertainments with the Edison Phonograph."* Latest Record Catalogue mailed to any Phonograph owner.

National Phonograph Company
22 LAKESIDE AVENUE, ORANGE, N. J.

New York	Chicago	San Francisco	London

I. C. S. Language Courses Taught With Edison Phonographs.

Latest Edison Gold Moulded Records — Now on Sale at All Dealers

9146 At the Old Grist Mill . . Edison Concert Band
9147 Lorna — *Song and Male Quartette* . . . Barrow
9148 The Golden Wedding (*Vaudeville*) Jones & Spencer
9149 Traumerei — *'Cello Solo* . . . . Hans Kronold
9150 Bye-Bye, My Eva, Bye-Bye — *Coon Song* . Collins
9151 Lily White — *Popular Song* . . . MacDonough
9152 I'm Old but I'm Awfully Tough — *Song* . Keefe
9153 Happy Heinie March . . Edison Military Band
9154 Girl from the U. S. A. — *Song* . . . . Gillette
9155 Nothin' from Nothin' Leaves You — *Song* Roberts
9156 Star, Beautiful Star . . Anthony and Harrison
9157 Romantic Overture Edison Symphony Orchestra
9158 Can't You See I'm Lonely — *Ballad* . Ada Jones

9159 Call Again, Calligen — *Song* . . . . . Favor
9160 Nigger Loves His Possum . Collins and Harlan
9161 With Flying Colors March Edison Concert Band
9162 Silver Threads Among the Gold —
. . . . *Song* . . . Marie Narelle
9163 Short Stories . . . . Frank Bush
9164 Sympathy — *Comic Song* . . . . . . Murray
9165 Killarney — *Xylophone Solo* . . . . . Benzler
9166 Starlight — *Song* . . . . Harlan
9167 As We Parted at the Gate . Harlan and Stanley
9168 Silent Night . . . . . Edison Male Quartette
9169 Good Night Waltz . . . .
For Dancing . . Edison Military Band

Thomas Edison.

WHY DO I ILLUSTRATE THIS PHONOGRAPH? Well, we had one of these "side winders" when I was a kid. My favorite records were "In My Merry Oldsmobile" and a record that the Reo Company furnished its dealers which gave a "bang up" sales talk on the merits of the Reo car. . . . I was a Reo dealer, so why shouldn't I have remembered it?—*Clymer.*

WARNING!

1906   THE
Long Distance Siren

A Perfect Warning Signal
Clears the Way
Gives You the Road
Prevents Accidents

EVERY DRIVER of a car has experienced the uselessness of the ordinary methods for securing the right-of-way.

HOW MANY ACCIDENTS could be avoided by a proper warning signal?

HOW MUCH ADDITIONAL PLEASURE one could enjoy if sure that the road was clear?

HOW OFTEN do you slow down because you fear the driver of the vehicle ahead has not heard that **insignificant "toot"** of the bulb horn you use?

HOW OFTEN accidents occur because you thought he did hear you?

HOW about the expense?

EQUIP YOUR CAR RIGHT

The Long Distance Siren

Beautifully finished in polished brass and aluminum. All wearing parts hardened and mounted on ball bearings. A quarter turn of the handle produces a volume of sound sufficient in every case to secure the right-of-way. The sound may be soft or loud, just as wished for. Any person can attach the Siren to the car in a few minutes.

STERK MANUFACTURING COMPANY
69-71 Wells Street, Chicago, Ill.

WRITE FOR OUR ILLUSTRATED BOOKLET

1906

"**Standard**"
PORCELAIN ENAMELED
Baths & One-Piece Lavatories
Add the Last Touch of
Refinement to the Modern Home

The charm of a dainty bedroom is greatly enhanced by the installation of a "**Standard**" Porcelain Enameled One-Piece Lavatory. Its gracefulness of design, its snowy lustrous whiteness, and its absolute freedom from crevices where dust and dirt can lodge, make it infinitely more sanitary and attractive than the old time washstand. With a bedroom so equipped the occupant is to a great degree independent of the bathroom. The cost is moderate—the comfort value enormous.

Our Book, "MODERN BATHROOMS," shows many beautiful Lavatory designs suitable for bedrooms with prices in detail. It also tells you how to plan, buy and arrange your bathroom, and illustrates many beautiful and inexpensive as well as luxurious rooms, showing the cost of each fixture in detail, together with many hints on decoration, tiling, etc. It is the most complete and beautiful booklet ever issued on the subject, and contains 100 pages. FREE for six cents postage, and the name of your plumber and architect (if selected).

The ABOVE "*Anona*" Lavatory, *Plate P-520* can be purchased from any plumber at a cost approximating $54.50—not counting freight, labor or piping.

CAUTION: *Every piece of* "**Standard**" *Ware bears our* "**Standard**" *" Green and Gold" guarantee label, and has our trade-mark* "**Standard**" *cast on the outside. Unless the label and trade-mark are on the fixture it is not* "**Standard**" *Ware. Refuse substitutes—they are all inferior and will cost you more in the end.*

Address Standard Sanitary Mfg. Co. Dept. 21, Pittsburgh, U. S. A.

Offices and Showrooms in New York: "**Standard**" Building, 35-37 West 31st Street.
London, England. 22 Holborn Viaduct. E. C.

THE May Queen has taken up the May Pole and gone. It is time for the boys in overalls and the women in aprons to get ready to dance to

THE HARVEST QUEEN

1906

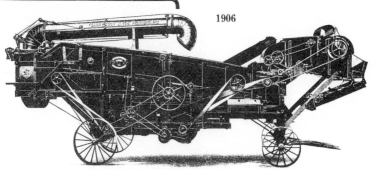

The Gaar-Scott Harvest Queen

Will give you a right merry dance, and you will have enough money left after paying the fiddlers, to satisfy you that threshing when done with Machinery built for business is a very fair business.

If you couple this Harvest Queen to a Gaar-Scott King Coal you will be the jolliest soul in the field. Our Straw-Burner Kings belong to the same royal family with the "Tiger" coat of arms.

Are you ready for the music to begin? If you are undecided about your King and Queen, a copy of our 1906 Catalogue and Tiger Truths will help you decide. Tiger Truths gives more facts and photographs from the field than you ever saw before in one bunch. The writers tell how they came to decide in favor of the Tiger Thresher Line, and how well they are pleased with their choice. Don't postpone your decision but write today.

GAAR, SCOTT & CO., RICHMOND, INDIANA

OLD KING COAL

STRAW-BURNER KING

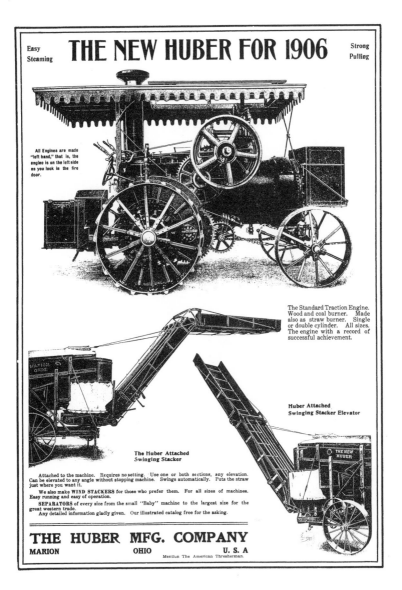

The Perfect Food Beverage

LOWNEY'S COCOA is an American triumph in culinary products. The most delicious and best made anywhere, or at any price.

THE WALTER M. LOWNEY CO., BOSTON, MASS.

Makers of Chocolate Bonbons and Chocolate Manufactures.

1906

First Among Pianos

By universal consent the Steinway Piano is accorded first place among the pianos of the world. Great artists and composers acknowledge it to be the supreme medium of instrumental interpretation; and among music-loving people, it obtains no less recognition as the fitting piano for the home. Piano-makers, regarding it as the one piano worthy of emulation, have taken it apart and examined it minutely in the hope of discovering its secret. But they have never reproduced

The Steinway

nor can they, unless it be possible to reproduce the generations of genius and devotion that have made it what it is—the first piano of the age.

In pianos, it pays to buy only the best; therefore, if you intend purchasing a piano, you can afford a Steinway. Our latest models, the Vertegrand at $500, and the Miniature Grand at $750, are wonderful piano values. It must be remembered that the life of a Steinway is much longer than that of other pianos. Should you be compelled to dispose of your instrument, the Steinway will always bring a higher price than any other make of piano. From any point of view, whether artistic or commercial, the Steinway is the great piano investment.

These pianos can be bought from any authorized Steinway dealer, with cost of freight and handling added.
Illustrated catalogue and booklets sent upon request.

STEINWAY & SONS
Steinway Hall
107 and 109 East 14th Street
New York

VERTEGRAND
PRICE $500

MINIATURE GRAND
PRICE $750

WHEN YOU SEE THIS SIGN ASK FOR A MASSAGE

USE
Pompeian
MASSAGE
CREAM
THE CENTURY'S TOILET LUXURY

1906

If you patronize a barber, remember that the Pompeian sign above in a barber shop is always proof that you can get a real massage there—that is a hand-massage with Pompeian Massage Cream.

If you shave yourself you can get a jar of the cream from your druggist, and with our book, perform facial massage correctly yourself. It is well to have a jar of

Pompeian Massage Cream

in the house in either case. After the day's work or sport, nothing is more refreshing than a good facial massage. Those whose occupation or sports expose their hands and faces to accumulation of dust and grime, find Pompeian Massage Cream the only thing that will entirely remove the soil from the skin. It removes the imbedded pore-dirt that soap cannot reach—and in addition, it increases the blood circulation, relaxes the muscles and makes the flesh firm and the complexion clear.

Do not allow the druggist to sell you an imitation, nor let your barber use a substitute—imitations do not do the work and may do harm. Look for the trade mark on the bottle, and see that the name "Pompeian" is there.

Your wife or sister will be glad to have a jar of Pompeian Massage Cream in the house. Most women today recognize the value of this preparation in maintaining a clean, clear, healthy skin. It contains no grease and makes the use of face powders unnecessary.

SAMPLE MAILED FREE

Send your name to-day—we also send a complete book on Facial Massage.

Regular size jars sent by mail where dealer will not supply. Price 50 cts. and $1.00 a jar.

POMPEIAN MFG. CO.
7 Prospect Street   Cleveland, Ohio

Men like Pompeian Massage Soap. A high grade toilet article, healing and refreshing, but not *highly* perfumed. It is for sale by dealers everywhere.

This is the jar the barber buys.

This is the jar the druggist sells for home use.

1906

Grand Opera Records *for the* EDISON PHONOGRAPH

WE ARE pleased to announce the issuance of a series of Grand Opera Records made by principal stars of the Metropolitan Opera House and by other prominent grand opera artists now appearing in this country and abroad. Hitherto, Mr. Edison has refused to permit Edison Records to be made by Grand Opera singers, preferring to wait until he could so improve his methods of recording, that the voices of great artists could be reproduced with all their characteristic sweetness, power and purity of tone. These improvements having been effected; the artists co-operated with enthusiasm, with the result that the first ten Edison Grand Opera Records, made by our Gold Mould Process, are a distinct advance over anything of the kind heretofore attempted.

Edison Grand Opera Records—On Sale at All Dealers

By HEINRICH KNOTE, Tenor
B. 1—HOCHSTES VERTRAUEN,
   "Lohengrin" . . . . *Wagner*
   Sung in German. Orchestra accompaniment

By ANDREAS DIPPEL, Tenor
B. 2—"ACH, SO FROMM," "Martha" . *Flotow*
   Sung in German. Orchestra accompaniment

By GUSTAVE BERL RESKY, Baritone
B. 3—"DI PROVENZA IL MAR,"
   "La Traviata" . . . . . *Verdi*
   Sung in Italian. Orchestra accompaniment

By FLORENCIO CONSTANTINO, Tenor
B. 4—"LA DONNA E MOBILE," "Rigoletto" *Verdi*
   Sung in Italian. Orchestra accompaniment

By ANTONIO SCOTTI, Baritone
B. 5—"VI RAVVISO, O LUOGHI AMENI,"
   "La Sonnambula" . . . . . *Bellini*
   Sung in Italian. Orchestra accompaniment

By SCARPHY RESKY, Soprano
B. 6—ARIA, "SUICIDIO,"
   "La Gioconda" . . . . . *Ponchielli*
   Sung in Italian. Orchestra accompaniment

By ROMEO BERTI, Tenor
B. 7—ARIOSO, "Pagliacci" . . *Leoncavalla*
   Sung in Italian. Orchestra accompaniment

By SIGNOR and SIGNORA RESKY
B. 8—DUET, "La Favorita" . . . . *Donizetti*
   Sung in Italian. Orchestra accompaniment

By ANTON VAN ROOY, Baritone
B. 9—"O KEHR ZURUCK,"
   "Tannhauser" . . . . . . *Wagner*
   Sung in German. Orchestra accompaniment

By ANTON VAN ROOY, Baritone
B. 10—"CHANSON DU TOREADOR,"
   "Carmen" . . . . *Bizet*
   Sung in French. Orchestra accompaniment

Signor Scotti says: "I have great pleasure in informing you that the cylinders which I sang for you are excellent from every point of view, and I *consider them as an absolutely natural production of my voice*. I must, however, tell you that the cylinder on which I sang the air from the 'Sonnambula' pleases me most, and I *certainly think it is the best of all I have ever heard.*"

In accordance with Mr. Edison's desire to make his Phonograph the musical instrument of the people, the price of these Grand Opera Records has been fixed at only 75c. each. Hear them at nearest dealer's. Write our Orange, N. J., office for handsome Grand Opera supplement.

National Phonograph Company, 69 Lakeside Avenue, Orange, N. J.

New York   Chicago   London   Paris   Berlin   Brussels   Sydney   Mexico City

OSTERMOOR

1906

Special Mattresses

Annual Clearance Sale of Surplus Stock

OUR surplus of especially fine French Edge Ostermoor Mattresses of *extra thickness, extra weight,* and exceptional softness, in the highest grade coverings, regular price being $30.00, will be closed out regardless of cost, to make room for regular stock, at the extremely low price of $18.50 each.

These mattresses are the very softest we can make, and are in every way fully as desirable and as great, if not greater bargains than the Special Mattresses we sold last year and the year previous at the same price. If you were fortunate enough to secure one of the same, you will fully appreciate the present sale.

Regularly at $30.00

Reduced to $18.50

The mattresses are all full double-bed size, 4 feet 6 inches wide, 6 feet 4 inches long, in two parts, with round corners, five-inch inseamed borders, and French Rolled Edges, exactly like illustration.

The filling is especially selected Ostermoor sheets, all hand-laid, and closed within ticking entirely by hand sewing. Mattresses weigh 60 lbs. each, 15 lbs. more than regular, and are far softer and much more luxuriously comfortable than regular.

The coverings are of extra fine quality, beautiful Mercerized French Art Twills—pink, blue or yellow, both plain and figured, or high-grade, dust-proof Satin Finish Ticking, striped in linen effect; also the good old fashioned, blue and white stripe Herring-bone Ticking.

Mattresses are built in the daintiest possible manner by our most expert specialists. They represent, in the very highest degree, the celebrated OSTERMOOR merit of Excellence and are a rare bargain both in price and quality.

Price, $18.$\underline{50}$ Each

We pay Transportation Charges anywhere in the United States.
Offered only while they last; first come, first served. The supply is limited.
Terms of sale: Cash in advance; none sent C. O. D.
Order direct of us or through your Ostermoor dealer.

Note:—Ostermoor Mattresses, regular stock, same size, two parts, cost $15.50 each. They have four-inch border, weigh 45 lbs., and are covered with A. C. A. Ticking. These French Mattresses cost $30.00 each, finish fully two inches thicker, weigh 15 lbs. more, have round corners—soft Rolled Edges—close diamond tufts— and beautiful high-grade fine quality coverings, and are much softer and far more resilient. Even if you do not wish a mattress now you should know all about the "Ostermoor" and its superiority to hair in health, comfort and economy. Send your name on a postal for our free descriptive book, "The Test of Time," a veritable work of art, 136 pages in two colors, profusely illustrated; it's well worth while.

OSTERMOOR & COMPANY

122 ELIZABETH STREET, NEW YORK

Canadian Agency: The Ideal Bedding Company, Ltd., Montreal

When ordering, please state first, second and even third choice of color of covering, in case all you like are already sold, as there will be no time for correspondence.

Reg. U. S.
Pat. Office

1906

W.S.B.

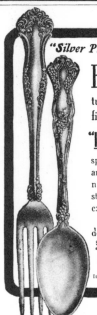

Snug for child and grandma

Her room and the nursery ought to be the most comfortable places in the home—always evenly warmed in any weather; but there is no even heating with uneven heaters, like stoves and hot air furnaces.

1906

AMERICAN & IDEAL
RADIATORS & BOILERS

radiate *soft,* uniform warmth throughout the building, with far less fuel. Our way of steam or hot water heating is a far-sighted investment—saves dollars.

Whether your house is cottage or mansion, OLD or new, farm or city, our outfit is adapted to it; and being practically indestructible it becomes a part of the permanent property value—unlike the short-lived stoves and hot air furnaces.

Health protection, lessened fire risk, freedom from dust and coal gases in living rooms, and labor-savings are also secured by use of IDEAL Boilers and AMERICAN Radiators. Youth to old age are all benefited.

Cost of outfit is paid for—for you—by the fuel-savings. Better read our booklet "Heating Investments," sent free. State kind and size of building to be heated.

AMERICAN RADIATOR COMPANY

Dept. 12   CHICAGO

NOT CHEAPEST BUT LEAST EXPENSIVE

Majestic

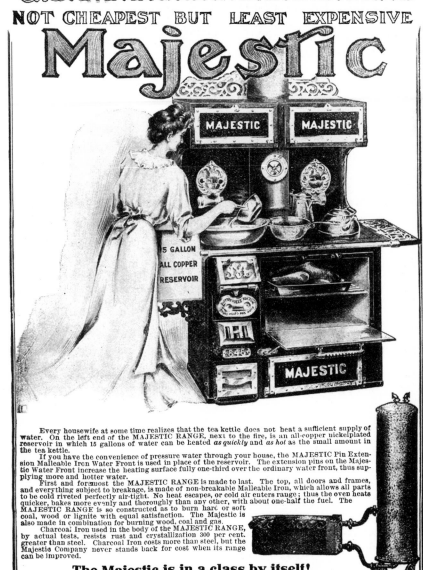

Every housewife at some time realizes that the tea kettle does not heat a sufficient supply of water. On the left end of the MAJESTIC RANGE, next to the fire, is an all-copper nickelplated reservoir in which 15 gallons of water can be heated *as quickly* and *as hot* as the small amount in the tea kettle.

If you have the convenience of pressure water through your house, the MAJESTIC Pin Extension Malleable Iron Water Front is used in place of the reservoir. The extension pins on the Majestic Water Front increase the heating surface fully one-third over the ordinary water front, thus supplying more and hotter water.

First and foremost the MAJESTIC RANGE is made to last. The top, all doors and frames, and everything subject to breakage, is made of non-breakable Malleable Iron, which allows all parts to be cold riveted perfectly air-tight. No heat escapes, or cold air enters range; thus the oven heats quicker, bakes more evenly and thoroughly than any other, with about one-half the fuel. The MAJESTIC RANGE is so constructed as to burn hard or soft coal, wood or lignite with equal satisfaction. The Majestic is also made in combination for burning wood, coal and gas.

Charcoal Iron used in the body of the MAJESTIC RANGE, by actual tests, resists rust and crystallization 300 per cent. greater than steel. Charcoal Iron costs more than steel, but the Majestic Company never stands back for cost when its range can be improved.

The Majestic is in a class by itself!

Call on your dealer and ask him to show you the MAJESTIC RANGE—first in cooking ability and in strength. Ask him for one of the MAJESTIC COOK BOOKS, FREE, containing many interesting and original receipts, or send 4c in stamps to us and we will see that you get one by return mail.

MAJESTIC MANUFACTURING CO.,   2052 Morgan Street,   **St. Louis, Mo.**

1906

Your Friends and Your Table

All who delight in giving original entertainments and little artistic surprises should learn how to use Dennison's Crepe Papers. This wonderful paper, in every color and hue is the very embodiment of art and from a few rolls can be created a veritable fairyland of enchantment. Many are the good-times that owe their delightfulness to the beautiful decorations, festoons, favors and table embellishing, that is easily wrought from

Dennison's Crepe Paper

It is the "art simple," costs very little and requires no experience whatever to design and fashion countless ornamentations that invest a social affair with the air of charming originality. Dennison's Crepe Paper is the only paper of suitable quality and the right texture for art purposes.

Dennison's Crepe Paper Napkins

The latest designs are superb in color effect. They take the place of linen at informal parties. They are dainty, serviceable and inexpensive. Napkins in special designs for special occasions—Flags for patriotic holidays, lily and orchid for Easter. Holly and poinsettia for Christmas, Hearts for St. Valentine's, Masonic, Delf and many others.

4 Books Free— Of Your Dealer or From Us

Art and Decoration—Tells and illustrates how to make everything with Dennison's Crepe Papers.

Napkin Book—Showing in color this season's designs.

Decorated Crepe Paper—Representing the newest color creations in this exquisite material.

Passe-Partout Book—Full instructions, with illustrations, for artistic Picture Framing.

If your dealer does not keep Dennison's Goods write to us and we will see that you get what you want. Address Dept. " 8 " at our nearest store.

DENNISON MANUFACTURING COMPANY,

The Tag Makers,

BOSTON, 26 Franklin St.
NEW YORK, 15 John St.
PHILADELPHIA, 1007 Chestnut St.
CHICAGO, 128 Franklin St.
ST. LOUIS, 413 North 4th St.

This Book

Tells how to beautify your home at little expense.

FREE

Don't wait—write for it now.

Consult this book and you'll save time, money and worry.

1906

Discriminating, home-loving persons are enthusiastic in their praise of this, the most elaborate and practical book on wood-finishing ever published.

Contains ideas worth $25.00 or more to discerning persons who enjoy and desire a beautiful home.

Write us now for above book, "**The Proper Treatment for Floors, Woodwork and Furniture**," and learn how easily and inexpensively you can beautify your new or old home. Gives confidential information from skilled wood-finisher of 23 years' experience about all kinds of wood, wood-cleaning, finishing and polishing. Tells how soft pine can be made to look like beautiful hardwood. Don't delay—write today. It's sent **free** by the manufacturers of

Johnson's Prepared Wax

"A Complete Finish and Polish For All Wood"

Unequaled for Woodwork, Furniture and Floors

Applied with cloth to bare wood or over dye, filler, varnish or shellac, it produces a lasting, artistic, sanitary finish to which dust and dirt will not adhere. It will not crack, blister, peel off, show laps, scratches or heel marks. Johnson's Wax is far superior to any other, one reason is that it contains the most polishing wax to the pound. Fine for preserving and polishing oilcloth and linoleum. Just try it.

This Mitt FREE

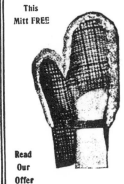

Read Our Offer

Johnson's Polishing Mitt, our latest device for polishing furniture and woodwork with our wax. Made of sheepskin with wool on, is open across the back and slips on hand. Sent FREE for label from one pound or larger can of Johnson's Prepared Wax. Remove label by placing can in steam or hot water.

Johnson's Prepared Wax **is sold by all dealers in paint**—½ lb. can, 30 cents; 1 and 2 lb. cans, 60 cents per pound; 4, 5 and 8 lb. cans, 50 cents per pound.

Write today for book and mention edition C3 Don't forget the label, either.

S. C. JOHNSON & SON

Racine, Wis.

"The Wood-Finishing Authorities"

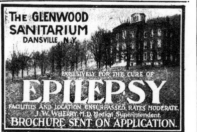

Go to California

There

Roses
Song Birds
Fresh Fruits
Sunshine
Comfort

1906

Here

Snow
Wind
Sleet
Slush
Bleak Skies
Chills

¶ It is an interesting, comfortable journey from Chicago or St. Louis to California by the Rock Island's

Golden State Limited

¶ The *quickest* train over the *shortest* route.

¶ It affords the highest type of luxurious travel facilities and runs by the warm winter way through El Paso.

¶ Write to-day, enclosing six cents in stamps for illustrated booklets of train, of trip and of California.

JNO. SEBASTIAN

Pass. Traffic Manager

CHICAGO

Rock Island
SOUTHERN PACIFIC
EL PASO
ROUTE
COMPANY

A very special rate for one-way colonist tickets, daily, February 15 to April 7—$33 from Chicago, $30 from St. Louis.

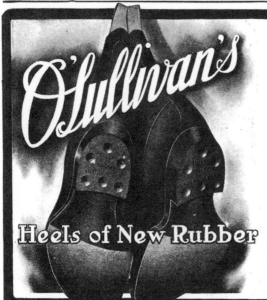

World's Shoe Record
How it was broken 1906

THIRTY-THREE YEARS AGO our first year's shipments amounted to $225,000.00. This year they are over *forty-two times* that amount. Thirty-three years ago we had seven employees—to-day 5000 shoemakers are busy the year round in our six great specialty plants—with a productive capacity of over *a shoe a second.*

American Gentleman Shoes are made by skilled workmen who make only the *finer grades* of shoes. The public appreciation of this brand is largely responsible for our gains of recent years.

For *12 years* we have held the *World's Record*, for sales by a single concern.

Sales for 1905, $9,522,835.04
Sales for 1904,   9,018,587.45
Gain, $ 504,247.59

We are the world's largest shoe manufacturers, —our shoes are sold in every civilized country.

Send for "Shoelight"

The Third Edition of our Style Book for Men is handsomer than ever. Be sure and send for it. Free.

STYLE 1027

A black *box calf* blucher, with welted heavy single sole, made on the comfortable 'Corliss' last. Staunch enough for showers and sleet, but not too heavy for comfort and flexibility.

American Gentleman

$3.50 $4.00
SHOE

ST. LOUIS, HAMILTON BROWN LARGEST SHOE CO WORLD U. S. A.

Makers

195

196

197

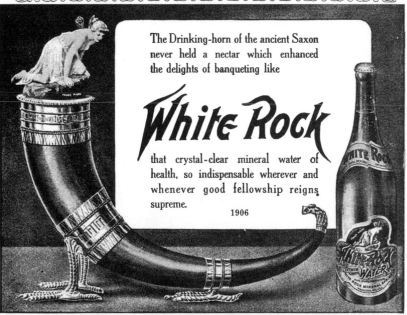

The Drinking-horn of the ancient Saxon never held a nectar which enhanced the delights of banqueting like

White Rock

that crystal-clear mineral water of health, so indispensable wherever and whenever good fellowship reigns supreme.

1906

PETER'S

THE ORIGINAL SWISS MILK

Chocolate

"High as the Alps in Quality"

DURKEE'S

1906

Peppers stuffed with Cabbage SALAD

is a deliciously tempting winter dish ; the peppers give it just enough piquancy of flavor to spur a jaded appetite. Use green sweet peppers, cutting a piece off the end to remove the seeds and partitions, then boil for five minutes. Next take the cabbage and, after shredding and liberally salting, let it stand for twenty minutes, then add half as much sliced potato as you have cabbage, season with our *Celery Salt* and stuff the empty peppers, then serve after pouring over all

Durkee's Salad Dressing

Hard boiled eggs may be used, if desired. Our dressing has a certain flavor, due chiefly to the use of the *best Olive Oil* (imported by ourselves), possessed by no other Salad Dressing.

Our handsome Booklet, "SALADS: How to Make and Dress Them," is the standard authority in its particular field. It contains many valuable recipes for a wide variety of delicious salads and is sent **free** on application to

E. R. DURKEE & CO. 534 Washington Street, New York City, N. Y.

The Girl in the White Cap

Every housewife should be acquainted with the Girl in the White Cap and her painstaking work in the Home of the 57.

In the spacious, finely-lighted, perfectly-ventilated Heinz Kitchens many hundreds of these neat, tidy, cheerful workers, daintily uniformed in aprons and caps of snowy white, co-operate with marvelously efficient methods and equipment in preparing pure food for the finest homes in the land. Why not let the Heinz Kitchen be *your* kitchen—and thus save a vast amount of work and worry in setting your table, at the same time retaining every quality of cleanliness, purity and home-made goodness. This is what is offered in each of the

HEINZ
57
VARIETIES

1906

Each year we welcome 25,000 visitors who come on all days and at all hours to marvel at the thoroughness, the precision, the care that attends every detail of the Heinz Way of doing things. Can you come? If not, let us send our beautiful booklet, "The Spice of Life," picturing and describing the largest pure-food kitchens in the world.

Your grocer sells Heinz products. Acquaint yourself with them by trying the delicious Baked Beans (three kinds), Fruit Preserves, Sweet Pickles, India Relish, Tomato Chutney, Ketchup, etc.

H. J. HEINZ COMPANY, Pittsburgh, U. S. A.

Copyright 1906 by Hart Schaffner & Marx

THE important thing to know about a rain coat is — Who made it? Our label's in ours; it stands for all you're looking for.

All-wool, rainproof fabrics; correct style, perfect fit, hand-tailoring.
Send six cents for our Spring Style Book.

Hart Schaffner & Marx   Good Clothes Makers
Chicago   Boston   New York

Swift's Little Cook-ing Lessons

Swift's Silver Leaf Lard

Swift's Little Cook

1906

Fried Chicken
Cut a Premium Milk Fed Chicken weighing about three pounds into quarters. Rub the pieces with pepper and salt and roll in flour. Melt in a frying pan enough Silver Leaf Lard to nearly cover the pieces of chicken. Heat the lard until it will cause a crumb of bread dropped in to almost instantly turn a golden brown. Then lay in the chicken and fry slowly until tender. When done remove and lay for a moment on cheese cloth or soft brown paper to absorb the grease. Serve garnished with parsley.
Swift & Company, U. S. A.

Swift & Company, U.S.A.

Dependable   1908   **Sizes and**

Economical   **Styles**

Simple and   **Adapted to**

Easily Operated   **All Uses**

I. H. C. Gasoline Engines

IT is not necessary to take any chances on the power you use. The record of I. H. C. gasoline engines is an open book. You know, or *can know if you inquire*, all about their satisfactory performance. There are many thousands of them in service, meeting all sorts of power requirements. Therefore, don't buy an engine at random. Be sure you are right. Ask any I. H. C. gasoline engine user about their efficiency, about their economy, about their simplicity, and ease of operation. You can depend on the judgment of the disinterested power users. Buying an I. H. C. gasoline engine is buying a known quantity. They are made in a large number of styles and sizes, including:

Vertical 2, 3, and 25-horse power.

Horizontal (stationary and portable) 4, 6, 8, 10, 12, 15 and 20-horse power.

Gasoline tractors 12, 15 and 20-horse power.

Famous air-cooled 1 and 2-horse power.

Famous skidded engines 2, 3, 4, 6 and 8-horse power.

Also a complete line of Famous mounting engines from 4 to 20-horse power, and sawing, spraying and pumping outfits and jacks.

Catalogs and particulars furnished by International local agents. Valuable book, "300 Years of Power Development" and catalog mailed direct from home office on request.

INTERNATIONAL HARVESTER COMPANY OF AMERICA, (INCORPORATED)
16 Harvester Bldg., Chicago, U. S. A.

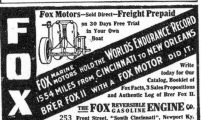

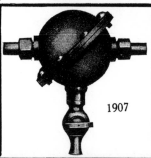
This gasoline strainer was probably the first filter to be used on any car. Dirt in the gas caused much trouble for pioneer motorists. Most early drivers used a piece of chamois for straining the gas while pouring into the tank. —Clymer

SIDE WINDOWS IN MOTOR HEADGEAR

In this illustration is shown the new motoring headgear worn by the women automobile enthusiasts of England. A window in each side of the bonnet is the suggestion of an Englishman who "also" feels that he has a right upon the highways, and fears for even the little chance of safety that has been left him unless his suggestion is accepted.

1908

Side Lights on Motoring

A CLYMER CAR !

Here is a car bearing my unusual name. I had no connection with this car, in fact never even saw one.—Clymer

206

Charles the Chauffeur 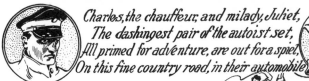 1907

Charles, the chauffeur, and milady, Juliet,
The dashingest pair of the autoist set,
All primed for adventure, are out for a spiel,
On this fine country road, in their automobile.

As they dash down the pike, without quaver or hitch,
The farmers in front of them take to the ditch,
And the cohorts that follow are trailing afar
Like the Netherby clan after young Lochinvar.

After climbing a long grassy slope, at the top
The pulsing machine has been brought to a stop,
For the silt of the air, and microbic flies
Have reddened the lids of milady's bright eyes.

And Charles, at the signal, has stopped the machine
And passed back the bottle containing Murine,
So milady leans back, and looks up at the sky
As the magic "two-drops" are dropped into each eye.

Now again they are off, at a forty mile pace,
With vision restored and new zest in the race;
And woe betide him who opposes their gait,
For he's booked for a serious tussle with fate.

The automobile, by some unwritten code,
Has won, in fee simple, all rights to the road;
And quite as true title indisputably, lies,
To the trite, but true saying, "Murine cures eyes".

MURINE. Is A Tonic For The "AUTO EYE."
SOOTHES AND QUICKLY CURES EYES
INFLAMED BY EXPOSURE TO STRONG WINDS AND DUST

I just had to show the illustration of this Oliver Typewriter, for it was standard equipment in the office of the Berthoud Auto Company, which I owned when I was 11 years old. I learned the "hunt and peck" system on one of these and I never "recovered" from it.—*Clymer.*

FORD "SOUND LOGIC" TALKS

QUANTITY PRODUCTION
MAKES HIGHER QUALITY POSSIBLE

1907

WE ARE NOW THE LARGEST producers of motor cars in the world, unquestionably. (Both in point of number of cars and in cash volume of business per annum.)

BUT THE QUESTION NATURALLY ARISES: "Must not quality be sacrificed in order to produce the quantities, and must not the low prices be made possible by the use of cheap materials, or work, or both?" Lots of successful men are unversed in the problems of manufacturing, though familiar with other kinds of wholesaling.

HERE'S INCONTESTABLE PROOF of our contention, "Ford cars are cheap only in price," and that quantity production not only does not necessitate sacrifice of quality, but actually enables us to put better materials, more accurate work in the making of a $600 car than has hitherto been practicable in American cars, even when sold at fancy prices—prices dictated not by quality, though that is the claim, but by antiquated methods and lack of facilities to do things the Ford way.

VANADIUM-CHROME STEEL is acknowledged by all metallurgists to possess qualities for meeting the conditions peculiar to motor car usage to an extent unobtainable in any other steel or alloy known. The price of this steel—due largely to the fact that it has been made only in small lots in crucibles or experimental furnaces of 2 to 4 tons—has made it a "commercial impossibility," as makers express it. Recently this special steel was brought a bit nearer by the discovery of a large deposit of vanadiferous ore. There was a race to get it. A certain engineers' association began to experiment—tried to corner the market.

AS USUAL FORD WAS FIRST. We didn't corner the market—didn't try to. But three weeks ago we made the first Vanadium steel ever made in 40-ton heats and by the open hearth process. Made several different grades each for a specific use, as springs, axles, crank-shafts, gears, connecting rods and frames. We are still the only American makers who use Vanadium steel in motor car construction.

AND FROM NOW ON Vanadium-chrome steel will be used throughout in all Ford models—runabouts as well as six-cylinder touring cars. Let others follow as soon as they can—we figure they're about a year and a half behind at present.

OUR DEMANDS FOR STEEL amount to 280 tons per month—four or five at least of our competitors would have to combine to make it possible for them to use Vanadium steel—and then the cost would make it necessary to charge you two prices for it.

BY THE WAY, we were the first and are still, so far as we know, the only makers who appreciate the wonderful results of scientific HEAT-TREATMENT OF STEEL PARTS AFTER FORGING OR PRESSING—the only concern in America who put every piece of steel through that "doubling-the-efficiency" process before machining. Ask about it—ten to one they won't know what you are talking about.

THAT FORD PRICES—Prices that stagger competition and leave a doubt even in the minds of buyers as to the possible value of the cars—are made possible by our methods of quantity production, is now conceded by those who know.

$2800 $600 $750

Ford
1907
Line

Six-cylinder Car
Touring or Runabout

Famous Model "N"
Four-cylinder Runabout

Model R, Four-cylinder
"Edition de Luxe"

PRICES F. O. B. DETROIT

FORD MOTOR COMPANY, FACTORY AND MAIN OFFICE, DETROIT, MICH.

BRANCH RETAIL STORES: New York, Philadelphia, Boston, Chicago, Buffalo, Cleveland, Detroit and Kansas City.

Canadian trade supplied by Ford Motor Company of Canada, Walkerville, Ont.

NOTE:

All ads appearing in this Scrapbook are of course void. They are reproduced not for the purpose of selling any merchandise, but for their historical interest. They afford an interesting comparison of the advertising methods of today and those in use earlier in the century.

SANDWICH
DUSTLESS CYLINDER SHELLERS

MADE IN THREE SIZES:
No. 2A, Capacity 400 to 600 bu. per hour
No. 5, " 600 to 800 " " "
No. 6, " 800 to 1200 " " "

Modern Extension Feeders
Chain or Belt, All Lengths

1907

Two Belt Hitches, right angle and parallel. Twelve foot Tilting Steel Plate Elevator. Powerful Suction and Blow Fans. Simple Shelling Mechanism. Never clogs. Indestructible. Mountings, wood or steel, as preferred. Cleans the shelled corn perfectly. Special Cylinder Sheller catalogue on application.

Sandwich
Spring Shellers

All sizes—all capacities. Belted and Geared. Mounted and Down. For Horse, Steam or Gasoline Power. Wood or Steel Mountings, as preferred.

No thresherman's outfit is complete without a Sandwich Sheller. Send for 62-page Spring Sheller Catalogue.

We also make a full line of

Horse and Belt
Power
HAY PRESSES

Sandwich Mfg. Co., Sandwich, Illinois

Peoria, Ill.   Cedar Rapids, Iowa   Council Bluffs, Iowa   Kansas City, Mo.

Please mention The Review.

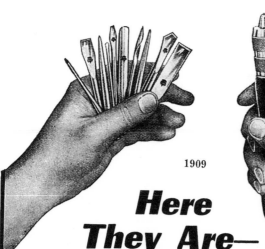

Awl and Tool Set
No. K-50
Price $1.50

1909

Here They Are— Which Do You Need?

Ten tools with the same handle for all. Just slip in the tool you want, the rest go inside the hollow handle, out of sight and out of the way.

A handy kit of small tools for home tinkering—fine for the boys—they can slip it in their pockets and have a kit of tools "right on the job" whenever and wherever they want them.

KEEN KUTTER
Awl and Tool Set

Contains 2 screwdrivers, 1 file, 1 chisel, 1 gouge, 1 gimlet, 1 countersink, 1 reamer, 2 awls, of the very highest quality. Tempered and ground as carefully and perfectly as all Keen Kutter Tools and carrying the same trademark and the same guarantee—money back if not satisfactory.

In buying tools or cutlery always ask for Keen Kutter and avoid disappointment.

If not at your dealer's, write us.

SIMMONS HARDWARE COMPANY (Inc.)
ST. LOUIS AND NEW YORK, U. S. A.

212

We Sell Thousands of Things
On 30 Days' Trial—On Credit

What We Sell On Credit

Furniture, Carpets
Rugs, Draperies
Stoves, Ranges
Silverware
Chinaware
Lamps, Clocks
Sewing Machines
Washing Machines
Baby Carriages, Etc.

8 to 14 Months to Pay

Our Mammoth Fall Catalogue is ready to send to you **FREE**. It pictures over 3,000 new-style things for the home. Everything in Furniture, Carpets, Draperies, Stoves, China and Silverware, Sewing Machines, etc.—every style and price. No store in America shows an equal variety. And no store can possibly meet our prices—that we guarantee. With this catalog you can sit by your fireside and see all the best housefurnishings the world has to offer. The pictures are perfect—some are in actual colors. And all things are sold on credit.

No Risk Whatever

If you see something you want, tell us to ship it, and we will send it on 30 days' trial. Then see how the article looks in your home. Compare our price with others. Use it a month before you decide about keeping it. If you are not satisfied with the article or the price, simply send it back. We will pay the freight both ways. You are under no obligation whatever. Isn't that immensely fair?

with us. No interest, no security, no publicity, no "red tape." We are originators of the open account credit plan. You can have, on the average, over a year to pay.

Don't imagine that credit costs more than cash, for it doesn't. We guarantee to undersell any cash house—mail order houses included. If you find that we don't, send our article back. The decision lies solely with you.

Don't Pay Cash

Three-fourths of the housefurnishings sold to city people are now sold on credit. They are paid for a little each month. It is useless and wrong to pay for such things cash down—things that last you a lifetime. The modern way is to have what you want and enjoy it, then pay for it as you can.

We bring these city credit conveniences to everyone everywhere. No matter where you are, or how little you earn, your credit is good

450,000 Customers

There are 450,000 homes now buying from us—buying over and over again. By pleasing them, we have made this by far the largest business of its kind. Our buildings now cover six acres of ground. Our combined capital is $7,000,000.

Our buying power is so enormous that we control the output of scores of factories. Our selling is done by catalog only, so our expense is exceedingly slight. It is utterly impossible for any concern to buy or sell lower than we. We guarantee a saving of 15 to 50 per cent.

Do you suppose we could do such a business as this if others offered equal advantages? Don't you know that these splendid methods—which have won us 450,000 customers—would win you, too, if you knew them?

Our Free Catalogs

Our General Catalog pictures and describes 3,000 new-style things for the home; furniture, carpets, rugs, draperies, and all kinds of household goods except stoves.

Our Stove Catalog shows 70 styles of Empire Stoves and Ranges, costing from 8½c up. Any one of these stoves will pay for itself in fuel saving before you finish paying us.

Cut out this coupon and send it to us. Do it now. We will mail either or both of the catalogs free. You will be amazed at the prices and our liberal terms. For your own sake, see what they are.

Solid Oak Upholstered Rocker
Richly carved, golden oak finish. Fabricord leather.
75c first payment, 50c monthly payments; total price, $6.85.

E-2490
Mutual Empire Steel Range

Six 8-inch covers. Blue steel body, asbestos lined; 14-inch oven; high closet; porcelain lined reservoir.
$3 first payment $1.50 monthly payments; total price, $21.95.

M-6002
Combination Bookcase and Writing Desk
Solid oak, golden finish; bent glass door. French bevel plate mirror
$2.25 first paym't, $1 monthly payments. Total price, $12.85.

M-6060—Gothic Iron Bed
Very massive. Best quality malleable iron and Bessemer steel. All parts framed and jointed.
75c first payment, 50c monthly payments. Total price, $4.95.

E-3824
Victor Empire Hot Blast
10-inch firepot. Burns all fuel.
75c first payment, 50 cents monthly payments. Total price, $4.95.

E-3794
Marvel Empire Base Burner
with 12-inch firepot. Self-feeding.
$3.75 first payment, $1.75 monthly payments. Total price, $24.95.

Cut Out This Coupon

SPIEGEL, MAY, STERN CO.,
815 35th Street, Chicago
Please mail me the catalog marked.

———— General Catalog.   ———— Stove Catalog.

Name ————

Postoffice ————   VOID

State ————

Soft steady restful light

Where reading and writing are to be done, and where an artistic effect is considered, no other artificial light is comparable to that of a good lamp.

But—lamp-chimneys that do not fit, cause endless annoyance from smoke and smell and flickering light.

MACBETH lamp-chimneys fit and insure perfect combustion, full illumination, and light of the soft, steady, restful quality that is the unique charm of lamp light.

I make a chimney to fit every style and size of lamp and burner, and my name is on it. Get the right one for your lamp. My Index, sent free, will tell you which one.

MACBETH lamp-chimneys are made of lamp-chimney glass that will not break from heat, and that is clear as crystal. My name is on every one. Address

MACBETH, Pittsburgh.

1909

1910

NABISCO
SUGAR WAFERS

The study of pleasing effects becomes almost an obligation when appetites are to be coaxed into action.

The serving of NABISCO Sugar Wafers with the dessert is an invariable rule with the successful hostess.

NABISCO SUGAR WAFERS may be had

In ten cent tins

Also in twenty-five cent tins

NATIONAL BISCUIT COMPANY

Cabinet
Glenwood 1910

Combination Coal, Wood and Gas Range

No Fussy Ornamentation or fancy nickel on the new Plain Cabinet Glenwood. Just the natural black iron finish. The Mission Style applied to a range.

The Broad, Square Oven

with perfectly straight sides is very roomy. The Glenwood oven heat indicator, Improved baking damper. Sectional top, Drawout grate and Ash-Pan are each worthy of special mention.

The Gas Range

attachment consisting of Oven, Broiler and Three Burner Top is made to bolt neatly to the end of this range when a combination coal, wood and gas range is desired.

For Wood or Coal

It Makes Cooking Easy.

Combination Coal, Wood and Gas Range.

Write for handsome booklet of the Plain Cabinet Glenwood Coal, Wood and Gas Range to Weir Stove Co., Taunton, Mass.

Write for Our Free Book on Home Refrigeration

This book tells how to select the home Refrigerator—how to know the poor from the good—how to keep down ice bills. It also tells how some Refrigerators harbor germs—how to keep a Refrigerator sanitary and sweet—lots of things you should know before buying ANY Refrigerator.

It tells all about the "Monroe," the refrigerator with inner walls made in one piece from unbreakable SOLID PORCELAIN an inch thick and highly glazed, with every corner rounded. No cracks or crevices anywhere. The "Monroe" is as easy to keep clean as a china bowl.

The "Monroe"

Most other refrigerators have cracks and corners which cannot be cleaned. Here particles of food collect and breed germs by the million. These germs get into your food and make it poison, and the family suffers —from no traceable cause.

The "Monroe" can be sterilized and made germlessly clean in an instant by simply wiping out with a cloth wrung from hot water. It's like "washing dishes," for the "Monroe" is really a thick porcelain dish inside.

Always sold DIRECT and at FACTORY PRICES, Cash or Monthly Payments

NOTE CAREFULLY The Solid Porcelain Monroe is so costly to manufacture that but few could afford it if sold through dealers. So we sell direct and give our customers the dealers' 50 per cent commission. This puts the Monroe within the reach of the MANY, at a price they can afford.

Sent Anywhere on Trial

We will send the Monroe to any responsible person anywhere to use until convinced. No obligation to keep it unless you wish to. The Monroe must sell itself to you on its merits.

The high death rate among children in the summer months could be greatly reduced if the Monroe Refrigerator was used in every home.

The "Monroe" is installed in the best flats and apartments, occupied by people who CARE—and is found today in a large majority of the VERY BEST homes in the United States. The largest and best Hospitals use it exclusively. The health of the whole family is safeguarded by the use of a Monroe Refrigerator.

When you have carefully read the book and know all about Home Refrigeration, you will know WHY, and will realize how important it is to select carefully. Please write for the book today.

Monroe Refrigerator Co., Station D, Cincinnati, Ohio

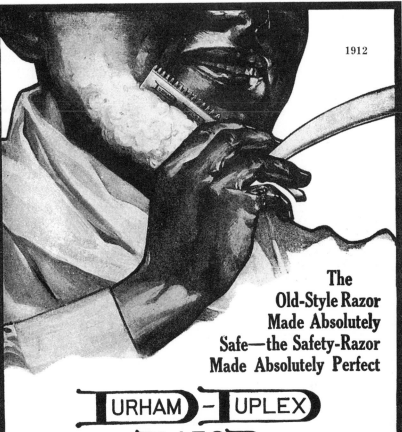

1912

The Old-Style Razor Made Absolutely Safe—the Safety-Razor Made Absolutely Perfect

DURHAM-DUPLEX RAZOR

Everything a Razor Should Be

If you use a "Safety" Razor, you'll like the Durham-Duplex Razor better because it has every good feature of the best "safety" razor and the additional advantage that it shaves with the correct sliding diagonal stroke—something hoe-like devices cannot do.

The Durham-Duplex easily and quickly shaves the toughest beard.

FREE TRIAL OFFER
The Durham-Duplex Razor is new, and therefore is not yet sold by all retailers, but we will send you the complete outfit upon receipt of $5.00, and if not entirely satisfactory, return it within 30 days and get your money back. Get one to-day.

Write for Free Booklet

If you use the old style razor, you'll like the Durham-Duplex better, because it has every advantage of the long blade, with the additional advantage of removable blades, making stropping and honing unnecessary; insures a sharp, keen edge for every shave. The blades can, however, be honed and stropped like an ordinary razor. New blades, 6 for 50c.

DURHAM DUPLEX RAZOR COMPANY, 111 Fifth Ave., New York

After the Last Taste   1912

"The Memory Lingers"

Post Toasties

Are made of carefully selected white corn;
rolled into thin, fluffy bits and toasted
to a crisp, appetizing golden brown,
already to serve with cream and sugar

Sold by Grocers

Postum Cereal Company, Limited   Canadian Postum Cereal Co., Ltd.
Battle Creek, Mich., U. S. A.   Windsor, Ontario, Canada

1912

The Most Perfect and Modern
An "Electric" Equipped with the
"Ironclad=Exide" Battery

The world has known many modes of travel, but just as it was left for the "Electric" to provide the perfect motor car for discerning people in cities and suburbs, so was it left for the "Ironclad=Exide" to provide the perfect battery for the "Electric."

The "Ironclad=Exide" positively has no peer in storage batteries for electric vehicles. It will give more miles with less expense and less attention than any other battery made. It requires minimum attention, gives good service in either cold weather or hot, does not quit on hills or in starting heavy loads, and can be recharged at a reasonable cost.

As a proof of unapproachable excellence there can be nothing more comprehensive than this;—the "Ironclad=Exide," the famous "Exide" or the "Hycap=Exide" Battery is used by every one of these prominent electric vehicle makers.

Argo Electric Vehicle Co.	Commercial Truck Co. of America	Ohio Electric Car Co.
Baker Motor Vehicle Co.	Dayton Electric Car Co.	Rauch & Lang Carriage Co.
Borland-Grannt- Co.	General Vehicle Co.	Standard Electric Car Co.
Broc Electric Vehicle Co.	Grinnell Electric Car Co.	Studebaker Automobile Co.
Champion Wagon Co.	Hupp-Corporation	The Waverley Co.
Columbus Buggy Co.	Kentucky Wagon Mfg. Co.	Walker Vehicle Co.
Columbia Motor Car Co.	C. P. Kimball & Co.	Ward Motor Vehicle Co.
		Woods Motor Vehicle Co.

When ordering an "Electric" or renewing a vehicle battery, insist on the "Ironclad=Exide." Write for the "Ironclad=Exide" book. The "Ironclad=Exide" guarantee is plain and straightforward.

THE ELECTRIC STORAGE BATTERY CO.
1888   PHILADELPHIA   1912

New York	Cleveland	Los Angeles
Boston	Atlanta	San Francisco
Chicago	Denver	Seattle
St. Louis	Detroit	Portland, Ore
		Toronto

812 "Exide" Distributors.

8 "Exide" Depots.

"Exide" Inspection Corps.

Accordion Music Wins Chimney-Sweep a Job

WEARING a topper and mounted on a motorcycle, beside which are tools of his trade in a side car, the chimney-sweep is a picturesque figure as he serenades potential customers in Margate, England, with an accordion. When trade is slack his music often wins him a job.

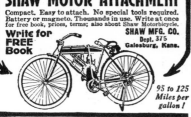
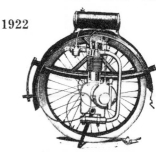

1912 Woodworth Treads

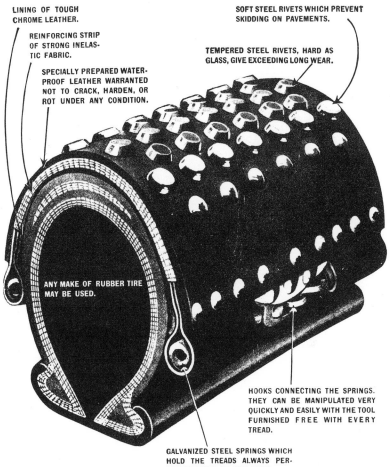

LINING OF TOUGH
CHROME LEATHER.

SOFT STEEL RIVETS WHICH PREVENT
SKIDDING ON PAVEMENTS.

REINFORCING STRIP
OF STRONG INELAS-
TIC FABRIC.

TEMPERED STEEL RIVETS, HARD AS
GLASS, GIVE EXCEEDING LONG WEAR.

SPECIALLY PREPARED WATER-
PROOF LEATHER WARRANTED
NOT TO CRACK, HARDEN, OR
ROT UNDER ANY CONDITION.

ANY MAKE OF RUBBER TIRE
MAY BE USED.

HOOKS CONNECTING THE SPRINGS.
THEY CAN BE MANIPULATED VERY
QUICKLY AND EASILY WITH THE TOOL
FURNISHED FREE WITH EVERY
TREAD.

GALVANIZED STEEL SPRINGS WHICH
HOLD THE TREADS ALWAYS PER-
FECTLY TIGHT ON THE TIRES.

Note the many valuable features of the new Woodworth Treads.
Note particularly the Quick-Adjusted fastening which enables one to apply the treads quickly and easily and which has been tested on over ten thousand treads, giving perfect results in every case. The coil springs hold the treads always perfectly tight, preventing any possibility of looseness to cause chafing or heating of the tire.
Note the hardened rivets where the wear comes—this means long life.
Note the treated leather—we guarantee this leather not to rot or become brittle under any conditions.
None of the features can be obtained in any tire protectors but the Woodworth Tread.
In spite of these improvements we have reduced the price to an extremely low figure.
Send for 1912 catalog showing the new prices.

LEATHER TIRE GOODS CO., Niagara Falls, N. Y.

This Timken-Detroit Rear ‹ is purposely shown with the rear removed, exposing the gears

Axle Anatomy is an Eye-Opener to the Average Owner

To know more about the rear axle will help yᴏ to understand one of the biggest problems of goᴏ motor-car construction:—

To understand the part of your car that does mᴏ different things than any other:—

The part that must be made of hundreds of sep rate pieces—and yet must be combined by perfe workmanship into a perfect unit.

Look at the Bearings in a Timken-Detroit Axle

You will find they are Timken Tapered Roller Bearings.

No others are used in the Timken-Detroit Axle

Timken Axles demand the *one* bearing that has the greatest capacity for vertical load, equal capacity for end-thrust, perfect adjustability for wear

The bearings in your car are so important, they have so many things to do that you should know more about them.

Timken Roller Bearing, with cap removed, showing the hardened and tapered steel rollers, held in position on the hardened-steel cone by the pressed-steel cage.

TIMKEN
AXLES & BEARINGS

Timken has been the pioneer in good axle construction.

First, there's the one-piece, pressed-steel housing, originated by Timken.

It has to be strong—a rear axle carries more than half the weight of the car and its load

It has a big, easily removed rear cap, so that you can reach the gears without trouble

Then there's the Timken power-transmitting unit—another feature originated by Timken.

All the gears—driving, pinion, and differential gears—are contained in this unit.

The entire unit is easily put in place, easily removed, and is completely assembled and tested before it is installed.

Timken accuracy demands the *grinding* of gears.

Even the finest gear-cutting r chines, alone, will not make gears quiet as *we* know they must be.

So Timken invented a proce designed and built a gear-grindi machine that corrects all the min inaccuracies left by the cutters

Gears, shafts, hubs, bearings, bra —all tell a Timken story

Every smallest piece—out ᴏf h dreds—is watched, tested, inspecte made perfect

Write for the Timken Prime No. D-7 "On the Care and Charac of Bearings," and No. D-8 "On Anatomy of Automobile Axles They will be sent free at your reque and will give you new knowledge these most important motor-parts.

THE TIMKEN-DETROIT AXLE CO., DETROIT, MICH.
THE TIMKEN ROLLER BEARING CO., CANTON OHIO

For more than fourteen years the Timken Roller Bearing Axle (made at Canton, Ohio), has been giving satisfactory service in horse-drawn vehicles

223

Now You Can Get Beer Without That "SKUNKY" Taste!

All you have to do is to ask for Schlitz in Brown Bottles.

Sunlight grows hops, but spoils the beer.

1912   **"Beer acted upon by light soon takes up the very disagreeable, so-called 'light taste,' and also a repulsive, skunk-like odor,"**

says no less an authority than the Wahl-Henius Institute of Fermentology, the scientific authorities on the subject. "Beer so affected," they say, "is offensive to the palate of most consumers."

Light starts decay even in pure beer. Dark glass gives the best protection against light. The Brown Bottle protects Schlitz purity from the brewery to your glass.

Why don't you, too, drink Schlitz? More and more people every year are demanding it.

We started in a hut. Today our agencies dot the earth. Our output exceeds a million barrels a year.

See that crown or cork is branded "Schlitz."

Schlitz
The Beer That Made Milwaukee Famous

29-M